Sweet Endings

cookies • cakes • pies • candy

Compiled by
FACS (Home Economics) Teachers

Editor
Gerry Murry Henderson

Graphic Design, Typography & Production
Mike Burk Production Services, Long Beach, CA

Visit us at: www.creativecookbook.com

ISBN 0-914159-23-2

1/110M062007/MBPS/DPS

Thank you for purchasing this book. The sale helps raise much needed money for school programs. And, a big thanks to the Family & Consumer Science and Home Economics Teachers for donating all the quality recipes.

TEACHER ADVISORY COMMITTEE

Kathie Baczynski
Mt. Carmel HS, San Diego, CA

Priscilla Burns
Pleasant Valley HS, Chico, CA

Neva Clauson
Lebanon HS, Lebanon, OR

Diane Cluff
Provo HS, Provo, UT

Jamie Davis
Redwood IS, Thousand Oak, CA

Carole Delap
Golden West HS, Visalia, CA

Peg Ellington
Yucca Valley HS, Yucca Valley, CA

Pam Ford
Temecula Valley HS, Temecula, CA

Maria Fregulia
Lassen HS, Susanville, CA

La Rae Hargues
Hesperia HS, Hesperia, CA

Debbie Harvey
Amador Valley HS, Pleasanton, CA

Gerry Murry Henderson
Temple City HS, Temple City, CA

Camille Hicks
Riverton HS, Riverton, UT

Reiko Ikkanda
So. Pasadena MS, So. Pasadena, CA

Mary Lash
Paramount HS, Paramount, CA

Jan Martin
Reed HS, Sparks, NV

Leilani Neiner
Mesquite HS, Gilbert, AZ

Ann Porter
San Luis Obispo HS, SLO, CA

Betty Rabin-Fung
Sierra Vista JHS, Canyon Country, CA

April Rosendahl
Chino HS, Chino, CA

Sonja Shumaker
Ayala HS, Chino Hills, CA

Karen Tilson
Poly HS, Riverside, CA

Betty Wells
Bidwell JHS, Chico, CA

Kathryn P. Whitten
Home Economics Education, Fresno, CA

Thanks to the following people for working hard to provide a good product and a simple, successful fundraiser. We couldn't do it without you!

Gerry Henderson, our editor, teaches full time and goes over every recipe to ensure there aren't any errors. **Sue Russell** and **Betty Rabin-Fung** spend many hours typing and proofing. Providing great customer service are **Roger Upperman, Ron Rouintree, Danny Hawes,** and **Jason Medina. Tim Campbell, Marc Trimble,** and **Grady Reed** travel throughout the Western U.S., helping teachers to be successful with their sales. **Mike Burk** designs the book, does the layout and makes it "printable". We're proud to print our books with **Jerry Bernstein** and **Delta Printing Solutions** in Valencia, California. And, a special thanks to **Shelley Herrema** for the "flip-over" book idea!

Sincerely,

Doug Pierce and ***Doug Herrema,*** owners, **Creative Cookbook Company**

To reorder this and other books, visit our website at www.creativecookbook.com, or use the re-order form on page 160.

Sweet Endings

Table of Contents

Flip This Book Over for
Great Beginnings

Table of Contents

Cover Photo for *Sweet Endings:*

Layered Cookie Bars

Makes 36 bars

3/4 cup (1- 1/2 sticks) butter or margarine
1- 3/4 cups vanilla wafer crumbs
6 tablespoons Hershey's Cocoa
1/4 cup sugar
1 can (14 oz.) sweetened condensed milk (not evaporated milk)
1 cup Hershey's Semi-Sweet Chocolate Chips
3/4 cup Heath Bits O'Brickle Toffee Bits
1 cup chopped walnuts

Heat oven to 350 F. Melt butter in 13 x 9 x 2-inch baking pan in oven. Combine crumbs, cocoa and sugar; sprinkle over butter. Pour sweetened condensed milk evenly on top of crumb mixture. Top with chocolate chips and toffee bits, then nuts; press down firmly. Bake 25 to 30 minutes or until lightly browned. Cool completely in pan on wire rack. Chill, if desired. Cut into bars. Store covered at room temperature.

Recipe and photo courtesy of Hershey's Kitchens

Brownies

Best Ever Chocolate Brownies

Makes 16

1 $^{2}/_{3}$ cups bittersweet chocolate morsels, divided
1 cup sugar
$^{1}/_{3}$ cup butter, cut into pieces
2 tablespoons water
2 large eggs
1 teaspoon vanilla
$^{3}/_{4}$ cup flour
$^{1}/_{4}$ teaspoon salt
$^{1}/_{2}$ cup walnuts or pecans, chopped, divided

Preheat oven to 325 degrees. Set aside 2 tablespoons chocolate morsels for drizzle topping. Heat 1 cup chocolate morsels, sugar, butter and water in small saucepan over low heat, stirring constantly, until chocolate and butter are melted. Pour into medium bowl. Stir in eggs one at a time, until mixed in. Stir in vanilla extract. Add flour and salt; stir well. Add remaining morsels (except drizzle morsels) and nuts. Pour into 8-inch square, greased pan. Bake for 33-35 minutes until wooden toothpick inserted in center comes out slightly sticky. Cool on wire rack. Place reserved 2 tablespoons morsels in small, heavy duty plastic bag. Microwave on HIGH for 20 seconds; knead bag to mix. Cut a small hole in corner of bag; squeeze to drizzle over brownies.

The chocolate drizzle on top makes for an elegant, as well as delicious dessert.

Sharon Chavez **Rogers MS, Long Beach, CA**

Chewy Triple Chocolate Brownies

Makes 12-24

1/2 cup butter
4 ounces unsweetened chocolate
4 eggs
1/2 teaspoon salt
2 cups sugar
1 teaspoon vanilla
1 cup flour
1/2 cup dark chocolate chips
1/2 cup white chocolate chips
1 cup nuts (optional)

Preheat oven to 350 degrees. In a small saucepan or double boiler melt the butter and chocolate; allow it to cool. In a mixer beat eggs, salt, sugar, and vanilla. Add chocolate mixture after it has cooled. Add flour until it is just incorporated. Pour into a greased 9 x 13 pan. Sprinkle the chocolate chips and nuts over the brownies. Press in slightly. Bake for 25-30 minutes. Cool, cut and eat!

This brownie is fabulous, always turns out perfect and is a crowd or kid pleaser. Amazing a la mode!

Priscilla Burns — Pleasant Valley HS, Chico, CA

Cookie Dough Brownies

Makes 24-36

Brownies:
1(1 pound 5.5 ounces) package fudge brownie mix
1/2 cup water
1/2 cup oil
1 egg
1/2 cup semisweet chocolate chips

Filling:
1/2 cup margarine or butter, softened
1/2 cup brown sugar, firmly packed
1/4 cup sugar
2 tablespoons milk
1 teaspoon vanilla
1 cup all-purpose flour

Glaze:
1 (6 ounce) package (1 cup) semisweet chocolate chips
1 tablespoon margarine, shortening, or oil
3/4 to 1 cup walnuts, chopped

Preheat oven to 350 degrees. Grease bottom only of 13 x 9 inch pan. In large bowl, combine brownie mix, water, oil and egg; beat 50 strokes by hand. Stir in 1/2 cup chocolate chips. Spread in greased pan. Bake for 33 -35 minutes. **Do not overbake.** Cool completely. In large bowl, beat margarine, brown sugar and sugar until light and fluffy. Add milk and vanilla; blend well. Add flour; mix well. Spread over cooled brownies. In small microwave-safe bowl, melt chocolate chips and margarine on medium for 1 to 2 minutes or until chocolate is just melted; stir until smooth. Carefully spoon glaze over filling; spread to cover. Sprinkle with walnuts, pressing down slightly. Cut into bars. Store in refrigerator.

Valerie Flores — **Sierra HS, Manteca, CA**

Easy Brownies

Serves 12

1 cup sugar
1/2 cup flour
1/3 cup cocoa
1/4 cup butter, very soft or melted
2 eggs
1/4 cup nuts (optional)
1/4 cup chocolate chips (optional

Preheat oven to 325 degrees. Butter the 8 x 8 pan. Put sugar, flour, cocoa, butter,and eggs in mixing bowl; mix thoroughly. Stir in nuts and/or chips. Pour into buttered pan. Bake for 25-30 minutes, until slightly pulling from edge of pan. Cool. Will still be soft inside.

These are my family's favorite brownie.
They are best warm and soft and a little gooey.

Susan Ballard — **Silverado HS, Victorville, CA**

Fudgy Figgy Brownies

Makes 16

1 cup semisweet chocolate chips, divided
2 ounces (2 squares) unsweetened chocolate, coarsely chopped
1/2 cup butter
3/4 cup sugar
2 eggs
2 teaspoons vanilla
2/3 cup flour
pinch salt
1 cup dried figs, stemmed and coarsely chopped

Preheat oven to 350 degrees. Grease bottom of 8 inch square baking pan. In medium saucepan, melt 1/2 cup chocolate chips, unsweetened chocolate and butter. Cool slightly. Mix in sugar. Whisk in eggs and vanilla. Stir in flour, salt, figs and remaining 1/2 cup chocolate chips. Spread into prepared pan. Bake in center of preheated oven for 25-30 minutes or until toothpick inserted in center comes out with just a few crumbs clinging to it. Cool in pan on rack. Cut into squares to serve.

Figs are among the most nutritious of all fruits. They are an excellent source of calcium, potassium, phosphorus, iron and fiber.
For more yummy recipes go to www.valleyfig.com.

Penny Niadna — **Golden West HS, Visalia, CA**

Graham Cracker Brownies

Serves 8-16

2 cups graham cracker crumbs, crushed (1 package + 1 single cracker)
1 can sweetened condensed milk
1 (6 ounce) package chocolate chips
1/2 cup chopped walnuts
1 teaspoon vanilla
dash salt

Preheat oven to 325 degrees. Grease or use nonstick spray on 8 x 8 baking dish. Combine all ingredients in large bowl. Stir until completely mixed. Spoon mixture into prepared baking dish. Bake for 30 minutes. Allow to cool and then cut into 2 inch squares.

This recipe is from a school friend who demonstrated it in 7th grade Home Economics. She e-mailed it to me after our 20 year reunion.

Mary Jo Cali — Arroyo Grande HS, Arroyo Grande, CA

Marshmallow Brownies

Makes 24-28 Bars

1 1/2 cups flour
5 tablespoons cocoa
pinch salt
1 cup butter
4 eggs
2 cups sugar
2 teaspoons vanilla
1 1/2 cups walnuts, chopped
1 jar marshmallow cream
Frosting:
1/4 cup butter
3 tablespoons cocoa
2 cups powdered sugar
1 teaspoon vanilla
1/4 cup milk

Grease 13 x 9 pan. Preheat oven to 400 degrees. Sift together flour, cocoa and salt. Melt butter; add eggs, sugar and vanilla. Add flour mixture, blend well. Stir in walnuts. Spread in pan. Bake for 15 minutes. Spread thin layer of marshmallow cream on top of brownies after cooling for approximately 10 minutes. Melt butter; add cocoa, sugar, vanilla and milk. Beat until smooth. Spread on top of brownies. Cool, cut into bars.

I obtained this recipe from my Aunt Mary about 20 years ago. They are impressive to look at and very good to eat.

Maria Fregulia — Lassen HS, Susanville, CA

Mint Chocolate Brownies

Makes 3 dozen bars

1 cup sugar
$^1/_2$ cup butter
4 eggs
$^1/_2$ teaspoon salt
1 teaspoon vanilla
1 cup flour
1(15 ounce) can chocolate syrup
2 cups powdered sugar
2 tablespoons milk
$^1/_2$ cup butter, softened
1 teaspoon peppermint extract
a few drops green food coloring
1 cup chocolate chips
6 tablespoons butter

Preheat oven to 350 degrees. In a large mixing bowl, combine sugar, $^1/_2$ cup butter, eggs, salt, vanilla, flour and chocolate syrup. Pour mixture into a greased and floured 15 x 10 jelly roll pan. Bake for 20-25 minutes. Allow to cool slightly. In a small mixing bowl, combine powdered sugar, milk, butter, extract, and food coloring. Use electric mixer to thoroughly combine. Spread mixture over top of baked brownies. Place in freezer to set icing. Melt chocolate chips and 6 tablespoons butter over a double boiler. Spread over top of frozen icing. Allow to cool or return to freezer. Cut bars using a sharp knife.

Try changing the extract flavor and food color for a different version. Use 1 teaspoon orange extract, 1 teaspoon orange peel and orange color; or try 1 teaspoon almond extract. These bars freeze well for later use.

Linda Falkenstien **Morro Bay HS, Morro Bay, CA**

Cakes

Apple Hill Apple Cake

Serves 10-12

2 cups sugar
1/2 cup oil
2 eggs
4 cups apples, peeled and diced
2 cups flour
2 teaspoons cinnamon
2 teaspoons baking soda
1 teaspoon nutmeg
1 teaspoon salt

Preheat oven to 350 degrees. In large bowl combine sugar oil and eggs. Add diced apples to mixture. In medium bowl, mix flour, cinnamon, baking soda, nutmeg and salt. Gently fold flour mixture into egg and apple mixture. Tends to be lumpy and not real moist...but way yummy! Bake in well greased bunt pan for one hour, check with toothpick; may need to bake an additional 10 minutes or so depending on your oven. Dust with powdered sugar.

This Apple Hill recipe from the Placerville area is a wonderful. "I need a cake in a hurry" dessert. I often use just one bowl... and sometimes my measuring is not as accurate as it should be... but the cake turns out wonderful every time! You can fold in a cup of chopped nuts at the end of the recipe... walnuts are my fav!... a cup of mini chocolate chips also add a little variety to the cake... major yummmm!

Dianne Lee Goldman **Cordova HS, Rancho Cordova, CA**

Best Carrot Cake Ever

Serves 10-12

Cake:
6 cups carrots, grated
1 cup brown sugar
1 cup raisins
4 eggs
1 1/2 cups white sugar
1 cup vegetable oil
2 teaspoons vanilla extract
1 cup crushed pineapple, drained
3 cups all-purpose flour
1 1/2 teaspoons baking soda
1 teaspoon salt
4 teaspoons ground cinnamon
1 cup walnuts, chopped
Frosting:
2 (8 ounce) packages cream cheese, softened
1/2 cup butter, softened
1 teaspoon vanilla extract
2 cups confectioner's sugar, sifted

To make cake: In a medium bowl, combine grated carrots and brown sugar. Set aside for 60 minutes, then stir in raisins. Preheat oven to 350 degrees. Grease and flour two 10 inch cake pans. In a large bowl, beat eggs until light. Gradually beat in the white sugar, oil and vanilla. Stir in the pineapple. Combine the flour, baking soda, salt and cinnamon; stir into the wet mixture until absorbed. Finally, stir in the carrot mixture and the walnuts. Pour evenly into the prepared pans. Bake for 45 to 50 minutes in the preheated oven, until cake tests done with a toothpick. Cool for 10 minutes before removing from pans. When completely cooled, frost with cream cheese frosting. *To make Cream Cheese Frosting:* In a medium bowl, cream together the cream cheese and butter until creamy. Mix in the vanilla; then gradually stir in the confectioners' sugar. Store in the refrigerator after use.

This carrot cake was a big hit with my friends and family.
The recipe comes from allrecipes.com.

Eurydyka Ciejka — **Rancho Alamitos HS, Garden Grove, CA**

Celia's One-Bowl Chocolate Kahlua Cake

Serves 10-12

1 small (8 ounce) container sour cream
2 eggs
1/4 cup oil
1/2 cup Kahlua
1 package chocolate cake mix
1 large package chocolate chips
shortening and flour to grease the pan

Preheat oven to 375 degrees. In a mixer, blend wet ingredients together until slightly blended; add the cake mix from the box and blend again. Lastly, add chocolate chips. Mix well, but do not over beat. Pour into greased and floured bundt cake pan. Bake for 50 minutes. This cake does not need frosting, but I usually either drizzle melted chocolate sauce over the top or sprinkle with powdered sugar. It is rich and delicious.

We make this cake whenever we need a last minute potluck dish. It's fast, easy, and simple to clean up, and everybody loves it. This recipe comes from a long lost friend from many years ago, Celia Wesenberg.

Amy Bean — Lompoc HS, Lompoc, CA

Cherry Swirl

Serves 12-16

1 1/2 cups sugar
1/2 cup butter
1/2 cup shortening
1 1/2 teaspoons baking powder
1 teaspoon vanilla
1 teaspoon almond extract
4 eggs
3 cups flour
1 (21 ounce) can Wilderness Pie Cherries
Glaze:
1 cup powdered sugar
1-2 tablespoons milk

Preheat oven to 350 degrees. Cream together sugar, butter and shortening. Mix in baking powder, vanilla, almond extract, and eggs until blended. Beat on high for 3 minutes. Mix in flour. Pour 2/3 of the batter into a greased 9 x 13 pan. Spoon cherries on top of batter. Drop the remaining batter over the filling. Bake for 45-50 minutes. Let cool for about 10 minutes and cover with glaze. *Glaze:* Mix powdered sugar and milk together; drizzle over Cherry Swirl.

Robin Lewis — Copper Hills HS, West Jordan, UT

Chocolate Espresso Cake

Serves 8-10

12 ounces bittersweet dark chocolate
4 ounces unsweetened chocolate
1 cup brown sugar
8 eggs, beaten
1 pound sweet butter, melted
1 1/2 cups espresso or strong coffee

Preheat oven to 350 degrees. Melt chocolates over a double boiler and let cool. Whisk in all other ingredients. Line a 9 x 2 1/2 inch round cake pan with parchment paper. Pour the mixture into the cake pan and place the pan in a water bath. Bake for one hour. Let the cake cool and then turn it upside down to remove it from pan. Dust with powdered sugar.

Joy Sweeney Aiello — **Portervile HS, Porterville, CA**

Chocolate Truffle Cakes

Makes 12

Truffles:
4 ounces bittersweet or semisweet chocolate, cut into small pieces
3 tablespoons heavy cream
1 tablespoon (1/2 ounce) unsalted butter
2 tablespoons flavoring of choice
(Grand Marnier, Amaretto, Raspberry liqueur, etc.)
12 fresh raspberries

Cake:
5 ounces bittersweet chocolate, cut into small pieces
5 ounces (1 1/4 sticks) unsalted butter, cut into small pieces
3 eggs, room temperature
3 egg yolks, room temperature
1/2 cup sugar
5 tablespoons, plus 1 teaspoon all-purpose flour
whipped cream and raspberries, optional

Truffles: Combine the chocolate, cream, and butter in a double boiler and let melt. When almost melted, remove from the heat and stir the mixture until smooth. Stir in flavoring of your choice and refrigerate until thick enough to mound on a spoon, stirring occasionally, about 30 minutes. Line a baking tray with parchment paper. Scrape the chocolate mixture into a pastry bag fitted with a #3 plain tip. Pipe eight 1/2 inch mounds onto the prepared tray. Place 1 raspberry in the center of each chocolate mound and pipe a little more of the chocolate mixture to enclose completely. Refrigerate until firm, about 15 minutes. *Cake:* Position a rack in the center of oven and preheat to 350 degrees. Butter 12 muffin cups. Line bottoms with rounds of parchment paper. Set aside. In the top of a double boiler, melt together the chocolate and butter. Cool slightly. In the bowl of an electric mixer fitted with a paddle, beat eggs, egg yolks, and sugar on high speed until tripled in volume, about 5 minutes. Add in the chocolate mixture and, on low speed, stir just until combined. Remove the bowl and fold in the flour, using a rubber spatula. Spoon a little of the batter into each of the prepared cups, top with 1 truffle per cup, and cover with the remaining batter. Place muffin tin on a baking tray and bake until edges of the cakes begin to pull away from the sides of the cups, 12 to 13 minutes. Let stand 10 minutes. Invert onto individual dessert plates and carefully peel off parchment paper. Serve warm with whipped cream and fresh raspberries, if desired.

Wendy Stewart — **Oakmont HS, Roseville, CA**

Decadent Chocolate Delight

Serves 12

1 (about 18 ounce) package chocolate cake mix
1 cup (8 ounces) sour cream
1 cup chocolate chips
1 cup water
4 eggs
3/4 cup vegetable oil
1 (4 serving size) package instant chocolate pudding mix

Grease the inside of a medium (4-6 quart), round crock-pot stoneware with butter or Pam for Baking. In a large mixing bowl with wire whisk, combine ingredients. Pour into crock-pot, cover and cook on LOW setting for 6-8 hours or on HIGH for 3-4 hours. Serve hot, or warm with ice cream. *Baking hints from Rival:* Do not over-beat the batters of cakes and breads. Follow all recommended mixing times. Do not add water to the Crock-Pot unless instructed to do so in the recipe. After cakes and breads have finished cooking, allow them to cool in the stoneware for 5 minutes before removing.

I had misgivings about baking a cake in the crock-pot, but this Rival recipe turned out great! Serve it with vanilla ice cream.

Ellen Gordon — Colton HS, Colton, CA

Double Chocolate Chip Cupcakes

Makes 12

3/4 cup butter, softened
1 1/4 cup sugar
2 eggs
1 teaspoon vanilla
1 3/4 cups flour
1/2 cup cocoa powder
1 teaspoon baking soda
1/2 teaspoon salt
1 cup milk
1 cup chocolate chips
powdered sugar

Preheat oven to 375 degrees. Line a 12 hole muffin tray with paper cups. In large mixer bowl, beat butter and sugar until light and fluffy (3 minutes). Add eggs and vanilla; beat well. Stir together flour, cocoa, baking soda, and salt. Add the flour mixture to butter/sugar mixture alternately with milk; beating well after each addition. Stir in chocolate chips. Fill prepared muffin cups about 3/4 full with batter. Bake 15-22 minutes or until cupcake springs back when touched lightly in center. Cool and sprinkle with powdered sugar.

These are rich and delicious! Enjoy!

Pat Freshour — Foothill HS, Palo Cedro, CA

Easy Chocolate Chip Pound Cake

Serves 10-12

1 (18.25 ounce) package yellow cake mix
1 (3.9 ounce) package instant chocolate pudding mix
1/2 cup white sugar
3/4 cup water
3/4 cup vegetable oil
4 eggs, beaten
1 cup sour cream
1/2 cup milk chocolate chips
1/8 cup confectioners' sugar for dusting

Preheat oven to 325 degrees. Grease and flour a 10 inch bundt pan. In a medium bowl, stir together the cake mix, instant pudding and sugar. Add the water, oil, eggs, and sour cream, mix until well blended. Finally, fold in the chocolate chips. Pour into the prepared bundt pan. Bake for 50 to 60 minutes in the preheated oven. Cake is done when a toothpick inserted comes out clean. Cool in pan for 10 minutes before inverting onto a wire rack to cool completely. Dust with confectioners' sugar before cutting and serving.

Heather Elick **Tulare Western HS, Tulare, CA**

Fresh Apple Cake

Serves 12-16

2 eggs, beaten
2 cups sugar
1 1/2 cups oil
1 teaspoon vanilla
3 cups flour
1 teaspoon salt
1 teaspoon baking soda
1 teaspoon cinnamon
3 cups apples, cored,peeled, and chopped
1/2-1 cup pecans or walnuts, chopped

Preheat oven to 375 degrees. Beat eggs and add sugar, oil, and vanilla. Stir. In another bowl, sift flour and add salt, baking soda, and cinnamon. Stir flour mixture and add it to egg mixture. Stir again. Add chopped apples & nuts. Stir. Batter will be gooey. Place in oblong cake pan, approximately 9 x 13. Bake for 35-40 minutes or until lightly browned. Test with toothpick in the center. Let it cool slightly and serve plain or top with whipped cream or ice cream.

This has been a family favorite of mine given to me from my mom, Solveig Costa. Everyone asks for this recipe whenever I take it places or serve it in my home. It's old fashioned yummy! It's great with granny smith apples but any kind will work.

Janine Walton **Etiwanda HS, Etiwanda, CA**

Funnel Cakes

Makes 6

oil, for frying
1 cup, plus 2 tablespoons flour
3/4 cup milk
1 teaspoon baking powder
1 teaspoon almond extract
1/8 teaspoon salt
1 large egg
2 tablespoons confectioners' (powdered) sugar

In a 10 inch skillet, over medium heat, heat about 3/4 inch of vegetable oil to 325 degrees. Meanwhile, in a large batter bowl using a wire whisk, mix flour, milk, baking powder, almond extract, salt, and egg until well blended. Holding funnel, made especially for funnel cake, pour about 1/4 cup of batter into the funnel. Over the hot oil, carefully release the trigger in the funnel to let the batter run out in a stream while making a spiral about 6 inches in diameter. Fry 3 to 5 minutes until golden brown, turning once with tongs. Drain well on paper towels. Sprinkle with confectioners' sugar. Serve immediately while still warm.

This is an old Pennsylvania Dutch Country recipe. This is a recipe that has been used in Home Economics classes for many years and I do not know who originally created it. It is by far the most requested recipe in my collection. Past students will see me in the store and ask for it. The almond extract is the most essential ingredient and when pouring the batter into the hot oil, it is best to connect the spiral to make a spider web design.

Cyndi Matthews **Etiwanda HS, Rancho Cucumonga, CA**

Individual Chocolate Lava Cakes

Serves 6

Center:
1/2 bar (2 ounce) 60% cacao bittersweet chocolate baking bar
1/4 cup heavy cream
Cake:
nonstick cooking spray
1 (4 ounce) bar 60% cacao bittersweet chocolate baking bar
8 tablespoons (1 stick) butter, unsalted
2 whole eggs
2 egg yolks
1/3 cup sugar
1/2 teaspoon vanilla
1/2 cup cake flour
raspberries and whipped cream

Centers: Melt chocolate and cream in double boiler. Whisk gently to blend. Refrigerate about 2 hours or until firm. Form into 6 balls; refrigerate until needed. *Cake:* heat the oven to 400 degrees. Spray six 4 ounce ramekins or custard cups with cooking spray. Melt chocolate and butter in double boiler; whisk gently to blend. With an electric mixer, whisk eggs, yolks, sugar, and vanilla on high speed about 5 minutes or until thick and light. Fold melted chocolate mixture and flour into egg mixture just until combined. Spoon cake batter into ramekins. Place a chocolate ball in the middle of each ramekin. Bake about 15 minutes or until cake is firm to the touch. Let it sit out of the oven for about 5 minutes. Run a small, sharp knife around inside of each ramekin; place a plate on top, invert and remove ramekin. Garnish with raspberries and a dollop of whipped cream.

Jennell Acker **Chino Hills HS, Chino Hills, CA**

Grandma Rose's Chocolate Sheet Cake

Serves 24

2 cups flour
2 cups sugar
1 1/2 teaspoons baking soda
1/2 teaspoon salt
1 cup butter
4 heaping tablespoons cocoa powder
1 cup water
1/2 cup buttermilk
2 eggs
1 teaspoon vanilla
Warm Chocolate Icing:
1/2 cup real butter
4 tablespoons cocoa powder
1/3 cup buttermilk
1 box powdered sugar
1 cup walnuts, chopped
1 teaspoon vanilla

Preheat oven to 350 degrees. In large bowl mix together flour, sugar, baking soda, and salt. In a saucepan, melt butter and dissolve in cocoa powder and 1 cup water. Bring just to a boil. Pour hot mixture over dry ingredients and mix together. Add in buttermilk, eggs, and vanilla. Mix well. Pour batter onto greased 12 x 18 x 1 inch cookie sheet. Bake for 15-20 minutes. Top with warm chocolate icing. To make icing: In a saucepan melt butter; add in cocoa powder and buttermilk. Bring to boil; then remove from heat. Add in the powdered sugar, nuts and vanilla. Make icing while the cake is baking. Very important to keep icing warm and spread on cake while both are still warm.

Grandma Rose made this cake for all our family gatherings. It is very simple to make and truly the best chocolate cake I've ever had! Moist and delicious! This icing is what makes the cake extra special! It melts in your mouth!

Ann Stark **Royal Oak Intermediate School, Covina, CA**

I'll Diet Tomorrow Cake

Serves 12-16

1 German chocolate cake mix
1 can sweetened condensed milk
1 jar hot fudge
1 large carton Cool Whip
2 Heath bars, crumbled

Bake cake according to directions in a 9 x 13 pan. While cake is still warm, poke holes on top with the end of a wooden spoon. Pour the can of sweetened condensed milk over the top. Warm fudge in the microwave until it can be poured over the top of the cake. Cover the whole cake. Refrigerate for an hour or so. Top with the cool whip and then the candy pieces. Step back and enjoy the praise!

This recipe was given to me by another AHS teacher, L. Lord.
Takes 2 hours to make, but it is easy and well worth it!

Julie Eyre **Alhambra HS, Alhambra, CA**

Instant Eclair Cake

Serves 12-16

1 box (1 pound) graham crackers, divided
4 cups milk
2 (3 1/4 ounce) boxes instant vanilla pudding
1 (8 ounce) container Cool Whip, thawed
chocolate frosting

Place one layer of graham crackers on bottom of 9 x 13 pan. Mix milk and pudding mix, following directions on box. Fold in whipped topping. Pour half the pudding mixture over graham crackers. Add one more layer of graham crackers, then the other half of pudding mixture. Cover cake with frosting and refrigerate for 24 hours.

Laurie Giauque **Olympus HS, Salt Lake City, UT**

Kitty Litter Cake

Serves 10-12

1 box spice or German chocolate cake mix
1 box of white cake mix
1 package white sandwich cookies
1 large package vanilla instant pudding mix
A few drops green food coloring
12 small Tootsie Rolls or equivalent

"Serving Dishes and Utensils:" 1 *new* cat-litter box, 1 *new* cat litter box liner, 1 new pooper-scooper. Prepare and bake cake mixes, according to directions, in any size pan. Prepare pudding and chill. Crumble cookies in small batches in blender or food processor. Add a few drops of green food coloring to 1 cup of cookie crumbs. Mix with a fork or shake in a jar. Set aside. When cakes are at room temperature, crumble them into a large bowl. Toss with half of the

remaining cookie crumbs and enough pudding to make the mixture moist, but not soggy. Place liner in litter box and pour in mixture. Unwrap 3 Tootsie Rolls and heat in a microwave until soft and pliable. Shape the blunt ends into slightly curved points. Repeat with three more rolls. Bury the rolls decoratively in the cake mixture. Sprinkle remaining white cookie crumbs over the mixture, then scatter green crumbs lightly over top. Heat 5 more Tootsie Rolls until almost melted. Scrape them on top of the cake and sprinkle with crumbs from the litter box. Heat the remaining Tootsie Roll until pliable and hang it over the edge of the box. Place box on a sheet of newspaper and serve with scooper. Enjoy!

This is the BEST cake I have found in a long time!
It is a blast to serve to friends for the "extra special" event!

Leilani Neiner — Mesquite HS, Gilbert, AZ

Lemon Cake

Serves 12-16

1 yellow cake mix
1 small package lemon gelatin
2/3 cup oil
2/3 cup hot water
4 eggs
Glaze:
1 cup powdered sugar
3-4 tablespoons lemon juice
2 teaspoons grated lemon zest

Preheat oven to 350 degrees. Grease a 9 x 13 pan. In a large mixing bowl combine the cake mix, gelatin, oil, hot water and eggs. Beat with an electric mixer for 2 minutes or until well mixed and thickened. Pour into prepared pan and bake for 40 minutes or until the cake begins to pull away from the sides of the pan. While the cake is baking prepare the glaze. Combine the powdered sugar, lemon juice and lemon zest. Stir with a wire whisk until combined and lumps are removed. When cake is done, use a wooden skewer or wooden toothpick to poke holes at intervals throughout the cake. Spoon glaze over the cake, allowing it to soak into the cake. Cool before serving.

This is a simple cake that always gets compliments!

Elizabeth Thornburg — Selma HS, Selma, CA

Mandarin Orange Cake-Torte

Serves 8

4 eggs
3/4 cup oil
1 package yellow cake mix
1 (11 ounce) can mandarin oranges, do not drain
Frosting:
1 (3 ounce) package instant vanilla pudding mix
1 (15 ounce) can crushed pineapple, drained
1 (8 ounce) container Cool Whip

Preheat oven to 350 degrees. Beat eggs and oil first, then add cake mix and beat 4 minutes. Beat in mandarin oranges with juice until oranges are crushed. Grease and flour 8-inch pans (3 or 4). Evenly distribute mix between all pans. Bake for 25 minutes. Remove from oven to cool. *Frosting:* Mix all ingredients well and spread frosting between the layers. Lightly frost the top and sides of torte. Refrigerate until serving.

This light and airy cake will be a hit at any get-together. Thanks to my mother-in-law, Helen, it has been a family favorite.

Virgie Panttaja **Sanger HS, Sanger, CA**

Mandarin Orange Cupcakes

Makes one dozen

1 1/2 cups flour
1 3/4 teaspoons baking powder
1/2 teaspoon salt
1/4 teaspoon cinnamon
1/4 teaspoon nutmeg
1/2 cup sugar
1/3 cup margarine
1 egg, slightly beaten
1/4 cup milk
1 cup fresh mandarin orange pieces, chopped

Preheat oven to 350 degrees. Sift flour with other dry ingredients. Cut in margarine. Combine slightly beaten egg and milk and add all at once to dry ingredients; mix only until moistened. Fold in orange pieces and break them up more if batter seems too dry. Fill paper baking cups 3/4 full. Bake for 20 to 25 minutes. Remove from muffin tins, allow to cool completely. Frost with your favorite frosting. Vanilla, cream cheese and chocolate are all great choices. The frosted cupcakes can also be topped with mandarin orange segments.

Marleigh Williams **Corning Union HS, Corning, CA**

Microwave Devil's Food Cake

Serves 6-8

1/4 cup butter, softened
3/4 cup sugar
1 egg
2/3 cup hot water
1 cup flour
1/4 cup cocoa
3/4 teaspoon baking soda
1/2 teaspoon salt
1/2 teaspoon vanilla

Using the electric mixer, cream together butter and sugar. Add the egg and water to the creamed mixture and mix well. Stir in the remaining ingredients and blend until smooth. Pour into a greased 8 inch microwave safe baking dish.

Microwave on high for 7 minutes, turning 1/4 turn every 2 minutes. Cover with plastic wrap and let stand for 10 minutes to finish baking. Serve immediately.

This is a great cake that can be made in a hurry.

Rick Griffiths — Riverton HS, Riverton, UT

Mississippi Mud Cake

Serves 12-16

2 cups sugar
1 cup oil
4 eggs
1 1/2 cups flour
1/3 cup unsweetened cocoa
1/4 teaspoon salt
2 teaspoons vanilla
3/4 cup nuts, chopped
1 jar marshmallow cream
Icing:
1/2 cup butter
1/2 cup cocoa
1/2 cup evaporated milk
3 3/4 cups powdered sugar (one box)
1 teaspoon vanilla
3/4 cup nuts

Preheat oven to 350 degrees. Cream together the sugar and oil. Add 2 eggs and beat; add the remaining 2 eggs and beat. Add flour, unsweetened cocoa, and salt; mix. Add vanilla and chopped nuts; mix. Pour into a greased 9 x 13 pan. Bake for 30 minutes. Allow to cool. Spread the marshmallow cream on top. For icing, mix together all ingredients and spread over top of marshmallow cream.

Look out, it's sweet!

Pat Smith — Kern Valley HS, Lake Isabella, CA

Molten Chocolate Lava Cake (Petite Gateau)

Serves 4-5

1/2 cup butter, unsalted
4 ounces bittersweet chocolate (Lindt)
2 eggs
2 egg yolks
1/4 cup sugar
2 tablespoons all-purpose flour

Butter and flour custard cups or specialty molds. (I use a heart for Valentine's Day and others for the holidays.) These will usually hold a couple of ounces, and this recipe will make about 4-5 of them. Preheat the oven to 450 degrees. Melt the butter and chocolate, but do not let it boil. Remove from heat and set aside. Beat together the eggs plus egg yolks and sugar, until light and thick. I use a wire whisk for about 5 minutes. Pour the now tepid chocolate mixture into the egg mixture and beat to mix. Quickly beat in the flour until just mixed. Pour into the custard cups. (At this point you can refrigerate for up to 24 hours. If you refrigerate, let it return to room temp before you bake) Put custard cups on a baking sheet and bake at 450 degrees for 6-7 minutes. The outside will be set up, but the top may still be slightly wiggly (technical French cooking term). Invert on plate, let sit for 10 seconds or so, remove custard cup. Sprinkle with powdered sugar, and surround with a fruit sauce of your choice.

The better the chocolate the better the product!

Faith Gobuty **Woodside HS, Woodside, CA**

Muffy's Crazy Cake

Serves 8-10

Cake:
3 cups flour
2 cups sugar
2 teaspoons baking soda
1 teaspoon salt
1/2 cup baking cocoa
2 tablespoons vinegar
2/3 cups vegetable oil
2 cups cold water
2 teaspoons vanilla
Topping:
1/2 cup chocolate chips
1/2 cup coconut
1/2 cup brown sugar
1/2 cup chopped nuts

Preheat oven to 350 degrees. Mix all cake ingredients together. Pour into a 9" x 13" pan. Sprinkle with topping ingredients and bake for 30 minutes. No frosting necessary.

A cake from scratch doesn't get any easier!

Julie Ericksen **Skyline HS, Salt Lake City, UT**

Pumpkin Cake

Serves 12-16

Crust:
1 yellow cake mix, save 1 cup of mix
1 egg
1 cube butter, melted
Center:
1 (large) can Libby's Pumpkin Pie mix
2 eggs
2/3 cup milk
Topping:
1 cup cake mix
1/2 cup sugar
1 teaspoon cinnamon
3 tablespoons butter, softened

Preheat oven to 350 degrees. *Crust:* Mix together ingredients and pat into the bottom of a 9 x 13 pan. *Center:* Mix together ingredients and pour over the unbaked crust. *Topping:* Mix together ingredients (I use my pastry blender) and sprinkle over pumpkin mixture. Bake for 45-50 minutes. Serve cold with whipped cream or serve warm with pralines and cream ice cream.

Great alternative to making pumpkin pie. Extremely easy.
This is a no-fail recipe. Anyone can make it successfully.

Ruth Dallas **Skyline HS, Salt Lake City, UT**

Pumpkin Pie Cake

Serves 12-16

Filling:
1 (large) can pumpkin
1 (large) can evaporated milk
4 eggs, beaten
4 teaspoons pumpkin pie spice
1/4-1/2 teaspoon salt
1 teaspoon vanilla
1 cup sugar
Topping:
1 yellow cake mix
1 1/2 cups walnuts or pecans, chopped
1 1/2 to 2 cubes real butter, melted

Preheat oven to 350 degrees. Mix all the filling ingredients together as you would if making a pumpkin pie. Pour into a 9 x 13 inch greased pan. Top with the DRY cake mix. Run a fork over the top to even it, but don't pack it. Sprinkle nuts over the DRY cake mix and drizzle melted butter on top. Bake for 35 minutes. Turn heat down to 325 and bake for 15-20 minutes more. Cool. Serve with whipped cream or vanilla ice cream. Refrigerate any left overs.

I use this dessert for my Advanced Foods Thanksgiving Dinner. I have probably given this recipe out to more people than any other! It is great, easy and fast.

Kathy Ewing **Johansen HS, Modesto, CA**

Pumpkin Roll

Serves 15-20

Cake:
3 eggs
1 cup sugar
1/3 cup pumpkin
1 teaspoon lemon juice
2 teaspoons cinnamon
1 teaspoon ginger
1/2 teaspoon nutmeg
3/4 cup flour
Filling:
1 cup powdered sugar
6 ounces cream cheese
4 tablespoons butter
1/2 teaspoon vanilla

Preheat oven to 375 degrees. Beat eggs for 5 minutes until foamy and light yellow. Add the ingredients, one at a time, beating after each ingredient. Spray a 15 x 10 inch cookie sheet with nonstick spray. Spread on batter. Bake for 15 minutes. Turn out on a powdered sugar tea towel. *Filling:* Blend all ingredients well. Spread filling on cake. Roll up. Wrap up in towel and plastic. Chill. Slice.

My students love this recipe and always ask if they can make it again.

Karyn Asch **Arbor View HS, Las Vegas, NV**

Quesadilla Cake

Serves 12-16

3 eggs
1 1/4 cups sugar
1/2 pint whipping cream
1/2 cup sour cream
1/3 cup Parmesan cheese, grated
2 cups Bisquick
1/2 cup milk
3/4 teaspoon baking soda
1/2 cube butter

Preheat oven to 350 degrees. Mix all ingredients. Do not over beat or it will rise over your pan while baking. Pour mixture into a greased 9 x 13 glass pan. Fill cake pan with mixture; allow it to sit 15 minutes before putting into oven. Bake for 35-45 minutes (check at 35 minutes).

Judy Hasperis **Reno HS, Reno, NV**

Raspberry Cake

Serves 8-12

1 package white sheet cake, baked
1 can Eagle brand sweetened condensed milk
1 cup water
1 small package of vanilla instant pudding
1 teaspoon almond flavoring
2 cups whipping cream, whipped
2 bags frozen raspberries

Cut cake into 1 inch squares. Place half of cake in a 9 x 13 pan. Mix Eagle brand milk and water; add pudding mix and almond extract. Beat together well. Refrigerate for 5 minutes while whipping cream. Fold cream and pudding mixture together. Spread half of cream mixture over cake. Layer half the raspberries. Layer remaining cake, cream mixture and last of raspberries. Cover with plastic wrap. Refrigerate several hours or overnight before serving.

Katie Borgmeier **Riverton HS, Riverton, UT**

Raspberry Coconut Cake

Serves 12

1 package white cake mix
eggs, water and vegetable oil according to cake mix instructions
3 cups flaked coconut, divided
6 (1 ounce) squares white baking chocolate
1/4 cup heavy whipping cream
3/4 cup seedless raspberry jam
1 can white frosting

Preheat oven to 350 degrees. Prepare cake batter according to package directions; fold in 2/3 cup coconut. Pour into two greased 9 inch round baking pans. Bake for 25-30 minutes or until a toothpick inserted near the center comes out clean. Cool for 10 minutes before removing from pans to wire racks; cool completely. In a microwave safe bowl, combine white chocolate and cream. Microwave, uncovered, on high for 1 minute or until chocolate is almost melted.; stir until smooth. Cool to room temperature. In a small bowl, combine jam and 1 cup coconut. Spread over one cake layer; top with second layer. In a small mixing bowl, beat together white frosting and white chocolate mixture. Spread over top and sides of cake. Toast remaining coconut; sprinkle over cake and press onto the sides of cake.

This is my new favorite cake. It makes a wonderful presentation and lives up to its looks. For a holiday cake with a snowy look, don't toast the coconut.

Kristine Carlin **Laguna MS, San Luis Obispo, CA**

Raspberry-Cream Cheese Coffecake

Serves 8-10

1 (3 ounce) package cream cheese
1/4 cup margarine or butter
2 cups packaged biscuit mix
1/4 cup milk
1/2 cup raspberry preserves
1 cup powdered sugar, sifted
1-2 tablespoons milk
1/2 teaspoon vanilla

Preheat oven to 375 degrees. Grease a baking sheet or line with parchment. In a medium mixing bowl cut the cream cheese and the margarine or butter into the biscuit mix until crumbly. Stir in the milk. Turn onto a lightly floured surface; knead lightly. Roll dough into a 12 x 8 rectangle on waxed paper; invert onto baking sheet and remove paper. Spread preserves down center of dough. Make 2 1/2 inch cuts at 1 inch intervals on long sides. Fold strips over the filling. Bake 20 minutes. After 5 minutes, frost with the combined powdered sugar, milk and vanilla. This drizzles over the cake. Serve with coffee or tea.

This is great for morning or after school meetings.

Joyce Cantrell **Rialto HS, Rialto, CA**

Ring of Gold Apricot Cake

Serves 8-12

1 cup butter or margarine, softened
2 cups granulated sugar
5 eggs
1/2 cup apricot jam
1/2 cup sour cream
1 teaspoon vanilla extract
2 cups all purpose flour
1 teaspoon baking soda
1/2 teaspoon salt
2 cups sweetened shredded coconut
1 cup pecans, finely chopped
1 (8 ounce) package dried apricots, finely chopped
Glaze:
1/2 cup apricot jam
2 tablespoons apricot nectar

Preheat oven to 350 degrees. *Cake:* Cream butter and sugar in a large bowl until fluffy. Add eggs 1 at a time, beating well after each addition. Stir in next three ingredients. In a medium bowl, sift together next three ingredients. Stir dry ingredients into creamed mixture. Fold in remaining ingredients. Pour batter into a greased and floured 10 inch tube pan. Bake 45 to 55 minutes or until a toothpick inserted into the center comes out clean. Cool in pan 10 minutes; turn onto a wire rack to cool completely. *Glaze:* Combine jam and nectar in a small sauce-pan over medium heat; stir until well blended. Pour evenly over top of cake. Store in an airtight container.

Just as the golden ring symbolizes never-ending love, our Ring of Gold Apricot Cake will be a sweet reminder of the enduring bond you share with a special friend. Sour cream and apricot jam give the desert a rich flavor and moist texture. This delicious token of your esteem is sure to be appreciated.

Diane Wolak — **Martin Luther King HS, Riverside, CA**

Strawberry Cake

Serves 12

1 box white cake mix
1 basket strawberries
1 jar Marie Callendar's strawberry glaze
1 container whipped white frosting

Mix cake according to box. You can make a 9 x 13 or 2 layer cake. While cake is baking, slice strawberries and stir in $1/2$-$3/4$ jar of glaze. Allow cake to cool completely. If you chose to make a 9 x 13, remove cake from pan and slice in half length wise; put strawberries and glaze in the middle. Replace the top layer and frost the entire cake with whipped frosting. If you choose to make a 2 layer cake, put strawberries and glaze on one layer. Leave room around the edges. The strawberries will spread out when you place the second layer on top. Frost with whipped frosting.

This is a great dessert that looks pretty and is refreshing on warm nights. It is usually gone in 2-3 days in my home.

Marshawn Porter — **Arroyo Grande HS, Arroyo Grande, CA**

Triple Chocolate Cake

Serves 8-12

1 chocolate cake mix without pudding in mix
8 ounces sour cream
1 small package instant chocolate pudding
$1/2$ cup oil
$1/2$ cup water
4 eggs
1 (12 ounce) package chocolate chips

Preheat oven to 350 degrees. Mix first six ingredients. Fold in chocolate chips. Pour into greased and floured bundt pan. Bake for 50 minutes. When cool, sprinkle with sifted powdered sugar.

This is my Aunt's favorite chocolate cake recipe!

Jill Enright — **Granite Hills HS, El Cajon, CA**

White Chocolate & Lemon Bundt Cake

Serves 10

Cake:
grated zest, plus 3 tablespoons juice from 3 lemons
3 cups (15 ounce) unbleached all-purpose flour
1 teaspoon baking powder
1/2 teaspoon baking soda
1 teaspoon salt
1 teaspoon vanilla extract
3/4 cup buttermilk, preferably low fat
3 large eggs, plus 1 large yolk, room temperature
18 tablespoons (2 1/4 sticks) unsalted butter, room temperature
2 cups granulated sugar
1/2 cup white chocolate chips, reserved
Glaze:
2-3 tablespoons lemon juice
1 tablespoon buttermilk
2 cups (8 ounces) confectioners' sugar

Cake: Preheat oven to 350 degrees. Spray 12 cup bundt pan with nonstick baking spray with flour. Mince lemon zest to fine paste. Combine zest and lemon juice in a small bowl; set aside to soften, 10-15 minutes. Whisk flour, baking powder, baking soda, and salt in large bowl. Combine lemon juice mixture, vanilla, and buttermilk in medium bowl. In small bowl, gently whisk eggs and yolk to combine. With hand mixer, cream butter and sugar at medium-high speed until pale and fluffy, about 3 minutes. Reduce to medium speed and add half of eggs, mixing until incorporated, about 15 seconds. Repeat with remaining eggs. Reduce to low speed; add about one-third of flour mixture, mixing until just incorporated after each addition (about 5 seconds). Repeat using half of remaining flour mixture and all of remaining buttermilk mixture. Scrape bowl and add remaining flour mixture; mix at medium-low speed until batter is thoroughly combined, about 15 seconds. Fold batter once or twice with rubber spatula to incorporate any remaining flour. Place 1/2 the batter into prepared pan, spread chocolate chips on top of batter. Top with the remaining batter. Bake until top is golden brown and wooden skewer or toothpick inserted into center comes out with no crumbs attached, 40-45 minutes. *Glaze:* Whisk 2 tablespoons lemon juice, buttermilk, and confectioners' sugar until smooth, adding more lemon juice gradually as needed until glaze is thick but still pourable. Cool cake in pan on wire rack set over baking sheet for 10 minutes, then invert cake directly onto rack. Pour half of glaze over warm cake and let cool to room temperature, at least 2 hours. Cut into slices and serve with extra glaze.

This cake does take time to prepare, but it is so moist and delicious that it is definitely worth the time.

Delaine Smith — **West Valley HS, Cottonwood, CA**

Candies

Almond Roca

Makes a very large batch

$1/2$ -1 cup raw almonds
1 cup sugar
$1/2$ pound (2 sticks) butter
$1/2$ -1 bag milk chocolate chips
$1/2$ -1 cup walnuts, chopped (optional)

Mix first three ingredients in saucepan. Cook over high heat stirring constantly until candy thermometer reaches 350 degrees (caramel-colored). Pour into large cookie sheet. Cover with milk chocolate chips (not semisweet). When melted, spread evenly with spatula (heat resistant). Sprinkle with finely chopped walnuts, if desired.

We make this every Christmas, and the students love it!
The serving size depends upon the amount of ingredients used.

Donna Baker **Redlands East Valley HS, Redlands, CA**

Candied Pop Corn

Makes a lot

2 large bags of microwave popcorn, popped
1 (12 ounce) bag of Nestles white morsels
1 tablespoon Crisco

Pop two large bags of microwave popcorn. Any brand will do. Remove any unpopped kernels. Pour popcorn into a large bowl. Melt the white morsels with the Crisco in a small saucepan, stirring continually. When melted pour the morsels over the popcorn and stir to coat. Let cool and enjoy.

This is so good, and so easy. My card group loved it.

Dian Abbott **Corcoran HS, Corcoran, CA**

Chocolate Chip Cheese Ball

Makes 1 cheese ball

1 (8 ounce) package cream cheese, softened
1/2 cup butter, softened
3/4 cup powdered sugar
2 tablespoons brown sugar
1/4 teaspoon vanilla extract
3/4 cup miniature semi-sweet chocolate chips
3/4 cup pecans or walnuts, finely chopped
Chocolate and/or Honey Graham Cracker Sticks

In a mixing bowl, beat together the cream cheese and butter until smooth. Mix in the powdered sugar, brown sugar and vanilla, Stir in the chocolate chips. Cover and chill in refrigerator for 2 hours. Shape chilled cream cheese mixture into a ball. Wrap with plastic wrap and chill in refrigerator for 1 hour. Roll the cheese ball in finely chopped nuts before serving. Serve with Chocolate and/or Honey Graham Cracker Sticks

This is my daughter's recipe and a favorite at family parties. Kids of all ages love it!

Camille Hicks **Riverton HS, Riverton, UT**

Cookies & Cream Fudge

Makes 36 1" squares

1 1/3 cups evaporated milk
3 cups sugar
1/4 cup butter
1/2 teaspoon salt
4 cups marshmallows, cut into small pieces
3 cups white chocolate chips
2 teaspoons vanilla
2 cups Oreo cookies, crushed

Generously grease a 9 x 13 baking dish. Combine milk, sugar, butter, salt in a large saucepan and bring to a rolling boil over medium heat. Stirring constantly, boil for 5 minutes. Remove from heat. Stir in marshmallows, white chocolate chips and vanilla. Stir quickly until melted and well blended. Quickly stir in the Oreo cookies and stir until well coated. Pour into prepared baking dish. Set until firm. Cut into pieces.

Linnea Howe **Pacifica HS, Oxnard, CA**

Easy English Toffee

Makes about 2 1/2 pounds

1 pound butter
3 cups granulated white sugar
1 pound dark sweet chocolate
1 cup almonds, chopped, roasted

Butter the inside of a heavy, high sided, 3 quart pan and the bottom of a pizza pan. Melt butter in 3 quart pan; add sugar, stirring constantly using a wooden spoon until golden brown or 290 degrees on a candy thermometer. Spread onto greased pizza pan and cool. Hit with back of knife to create cracks in toffee. Melt chocolate in a double boiler; pour over the top of the toffee. Sprinkle with almonds. Place in refrigerator to set. Break into bite sized pieces.

Jill Sweet Gregory **Santa Paula HS, Santa Paula, CA**

Endless Choices Chocolate Truffles

Makes 2 dozen

1 package Oreo cookies, finely ground
1 (8 ounce) package cream cheese, softened
2 cups semisweet chocolate
2 tablespoons shortening
Toppings: cocoa, sprinkles, nuts, toffee pieces, coconut, white chocolate, etc.

Finely grind cookies in a food processor or use a rolling pin on a Ziploc bag filled with the cookies. Stir together cookie crumbs and cream cheese; form into 1 inch balls. Place on waxed paper and chill in the refrigerator. Melt the chocolate and shortening in the microwave for 1 minute. Stir, then melt for another minute. Stir until melted and glossy. Dip chilled truffles into chocolate.

Walnut Mint Bars

Makes 24-36

1/2 cup (1 stick) plus 2 tablespoons margarine, divided
1-1/2 cups vanilla wafer crumbs (about 45 wafers)
1 cup chopped walnuts
1/3 cup powdered sugar
1/3 cup Hershey's Semi-Sweet Chocolate Chips
1 package (8 oz.) cream cheese, softened
1 tablespoon cornstarch
1 can (14 oz.) sweetened condensed milk (not evaporated milk)
1 egg
1-1/2 teaspoons peppermint extract or 1 tablespoon green creme de menthe
Green food color (optional)
Chocolate Drizzle (recipe follows)

Heat oven to 350°F. Melt 1/2 cup margarine in medium saucepan; stir in crumbs, walnuts, sugar and cocoa. Press firmly on bottom of ungreased 13x9x2-inch baking pan. Beat cream cheese, remaining 2 tablespoons margarine and cornstarch in small bowl until fluffy. Gradually beat in sweetened condensed milk then egg, peppermint extract and food color, if desired. Pour evenly into prepared pan. Bake 25 minutes or until center is set. Cool. Drizzle "Chocolate Drizzle" over top. Refrigerate until thoroughly chilled. Cut into bars. Store covered in refrigerator. 24 to 36 bars. *Chocolate Drizzle:* Melt 1 cup Hershey's Semi-Sweet Chocolate Chips with 1-1/2 teaspoons shortening (do not use butter, margarine or oil).

Recipes and photos courtesy of Hershey's Kitchens

Peppermint Pattie Chocolate Cheesecake

Serves 10-12

Chocolate Crumb Crust:
3 packages (8 oz. each) cream cheese, softened
1 cup sugar
1/4 cup Hershey's Special Dark Cocoa
1 teaspoon vanilla extract
4 eggs
1/4 cup heavy cream
1 1/3 cups (8-oz. pkg.) York Mini Peppermint Patties, divided
Sweetened whipped cream or whipped topping

Prepare Chocolate Crumb Crust. Heat oven to 350°:F. Beat cream cheese and sugar in large bowl until smooth. Blend in cocoa and vanilla. Gradually beat in eggs and heavy cream, beating until well blended. Pour 2 cups batter in prepared crust. Place 1/4 cup peppermint patties in small microwave-safe bowl. Microwave at MEDIUM (50%) 1 minute; stir. If necessary, microwave at MEDIUM an additional 15 seconds at a time, stirring after each heating, until pieces are melted and smooth when stirred. Place 1 cup cheesecake batter into separate bowl; blend in melted chocolate mixture. Carefully spoon over cheesecake batter in pan. Coarsely chop 3/4 cup peppermint patties; sprinkle over surface. Spoon remaining batter over patties; spread to cover. Bake 50 to 55 minutes or until center is almost set. Remove from oven to wire rack. With knife, loosen cake from side of pan. Cool to room temperature. Cover; refrigerate several hours or until cold. Garnish with whipped cream and remaining peppermint patties. Cover; refrigerate leftovers. 10 to 12 servings. *Chocolate Crumb Crust:* Stir together 1 1/2 cups vanilla wafer crumbs (about 45 cookies), 1/4 cup Hershey's Special Dark Cocoa, 1/4 cup powdered sugar and 1/4 cup (1/2 stick) melted butter or margarine. Press mixture onto bottom and 1 inch up sides of 9-inch springform pan.

Walnut Mint Bars

Peppermint Pattie Chocolate Cheesecake

Brownie Caramel Pecan Bars

Double Peanut Butter Paisley Brownies

Brownie Caramel Pecan Bars

Makes 16 bars

1/2 cup sugar
2 tablespoons butter or margarine
2 tablespoons water
2 cups (12-oz. pkg.) Hershey's Semi-Sweet Chocolate Chips, divided
2 eggs
1 teaspoon vanilla extract
2/3 cup all-purpose flour
1/4 teaspoon baking soda
1/4 teaspoon salt
Caramel Topping (recipe below):
1 cup pecan pieces

Heat oven to 350°F. Line 9-inch square baking pan with foil, extending foil over edges of pan; grease and flour foil. Combine sugar, butter and water in medium saucepan; cook over low heat, stirring constantly, until mixture boils. Remove from heat; immediately add 1 cup chocolate chips, stirring until melted. Beat in eggs and vanilla until well blended. Stir together flour, baking soda and salt; stir into chocolate mixture. Spread batter into prepared pan. Bake 15 to 20 minutes or until brownies begin to pull away from sides of pan. Meanwhile, prepare Caramel Topping. Remove brownies from oven; immediately and carefully spread with caramel topping. Sprinkle remaining 1 cup chips and pecans over topping; lightly press into topping. Cool completely in pan on wire rack, being careful not to disturb chips while soft. Lift out of pan; cut into bars. *Caramel Topping:* Remove wrappers from 25 caramel candies. Combine 2 tablespoons butter or margarine, caramels and 1 tablespoon milk in medium microwave-safe bowl. Microwave at HIGH (100%) 1 minute; stir. Microwave an additional 1 to 2 minutes, stirring every 30 seconds, or until caramels are melted and mixture is smooth when stirred. Use immediately.

Recipes and photos courtesy of Hershey's Kitchens

Double Peanut Butter Paisley Brownies

Makes 36

1/2 cup (1 stick) butter or margarine, softened
1/4 cup Reese's Creamy Peanut Butter
1 cup granulated sugar
1 cup packed light brown sugar
3 eggs
1 teaspoon vanilla extract
2 cups all-purpose flour
2 teaspoons baking powder
1/4 teaspoon salt
1 2/3 cups (10-oz. pkg.) Reese's Peanut Butter Chips
1/2 cup Hershey's Syrup

Heat oven to 350°F. Grease 13 x 9 x 2-inch baking pan. Beat butter and peanut butter in large bowl. Add sugar and brown sugar; beat well. Add eggs, one at a time, beating well after each addition. Blend in vanilla. Stir together flour, baking powder and salt; mix into peanut butter mixture, blending well. Stir in peanut butter chips. Spread half of batter into prepared pan; spoon syrup over top. Carefully top with remaining batter; swirl with metal spatula or knife for marbled effect. Bake 35 to 40 minutes or until lightly browned. Cool completely in pan on wire rack. Cut into squares.

Roll in your choice of toppings and place truffles on waxed paper to harden. Chill for a few hours before serving. Keep chilled.

Fanua Matagi — Chino HS, Chino, CA

English Toffee

Makes 1 pound

1 stick of butter
1/2 cup sugar
1 tablespoon water
1/4 cup slivered almonds
1/2 teaspoon vanilla
2 (1.55 ounce) chocolate bars
1 tablespoon ground almonds

Cook butter, sugar and water in saucepan, stirring constantly with a wooden spoon for approximately 8-10 minutes. Use medium high heat. Be careful not to scorch; should be medium tan color. Add almonds and cook a minute longer. Use the cold water test; candy should be at the hard crack stage. Take off the heat and add vanilla. Spread candy on cookie sheet. Spread melted chocolate bars on candy. Sprinkle ground almonds on top of toffee.

The best ever! Great for the holidays!

Anne Silveira — Shasta HS, Redding, CA

Homemade Marshmallows

Makes 20-40

3 packages unflavored gelatin (2 tablespoons)
1 1/2 cups sugar
1 cup light corn syrup
1/4 teaspoon salt (preferably Kosher)
1 cup cold water, divided
1 tablespoon pure vanilla extract
Confectioners' sugar for dusting (about 2 cups)

Pour the gelatin into the bowl of an electric mixer fitted with the whisk attachment. Also, fill a tall glass with hot water and put aside, to stick the candy thermometer in later. Meanwhile, combine the sugar, corn syrup, salt, and 1/2 cup water in a small saucepan and cook over medium-high heat until candy thermometer reads 240 degrees, called "soft ball stage" in candy making. Right before syrup reaches 240 degrees, pour cup cold water into the mixer bowl with the gelatin. When syrup is ready, take thermometer out and put thermometer in glass of hot water. Start the mixer at low speed and slowly, and carefully, pour in the hot syrup. When all the syrup has been added, turn the mixer on high and let whisk for about 10-15 minutes, until the mixture is very white, thick, and fluffy. Add in vanilla and mix in thoroughly. Meanwhile, with a sieve or sifter, generously dust a 9 x 13 inch baking pan with powdered sugar. When marshmallow is ready, pour into pan, dust with more powdered sugar and pat out to smooth. Allow to stand overnight to dry out. Cut into squares with scissors or into shapes with cookie cutters. Roll in additional powdered sugar if needed.

This is a fun recipe to serve along with homemade hot cocoa on a chilly night!

Anne Johnson Rio Norte JHS, Santa Clarita, CA

Mounds & Almond Joys

Makes 18

1 large package flaked coconut
1 heaping tablespoon flour
1/3 cup water
2/3 cup light corn syrup
pinch of salt
dipping chocolate
almonds (optional)

Combine coconut and flour in a large bowl. In a saucepan, combine water, corn syrup and salt. Cook to medium soft ball stage when candy thermometer reads 240 degrees. Pour syrup over coconut; stir to coat coconut mixture with syrup. Press into a buttered 9 x 9 pan. Let cool. Cut into squares, dip into chocolate. For almond joys top each square with an almond before dipping with chocolate.

If you like mound or almond joy candy, you will love these. They are easy, quick, and a crowd pleaser. This has been a standard part of my candy unit for thirty years!

April Rosendahl Chino HS, Chino, CA

Outrageous Coconut Balls

Makes 3-4 dozen

1 box white cake mix
1/2 teaspoon coconut extract
1/2 teaspoon almond extract
1/2 cup flake coconut
1 (16 ounce) can cream cheese frosting
16 ounces white or chocolate morsels (chocolate chips)
1 tablespoon solid shortening

Make cake in 9 x 13 inch baking pan according to directions, adding coconut and almond extract. Cool and crumble into a big bowl; add coconut flakes and toss with hands. Add cream cheese frosting and mix with hands. Chill in refrigerator and then form into balls. Keep refrigerated until ready to dip in chocolate. Melt white or chocolate chips with shortening in microwave. Dip each ball in chocolate mixture and place on wax paper.

Wow! These are always popular. White chocolate are most people's favorite. The white cake with 2 added extracts makes a great birthday cake.

Marilyn Bankhead San Marcos HS, San Marcos, CA

Sugared Pecans

Makes 1 pound

1 egg white
1 tablespoon water
1 cup sugar
1 teaspoon salt
1 teaspoon cinnamon
1 pound pecan halves

Preheat oven to 300 degrees. Beat egg white with water into a froth. In a large, zip closure plastic bag, combine sugar, salt, and cinnamon. Dip pecans in the egg white. Place coated pecans in the bag containing the sugar mixture and shake, coating well. Place on a well greased shallow baking sheet. Bake for 40 minutes or until egg white is dry. Stir every 10 minutes. Cool on waxed paper.

These sugared nuts are great as an appetizer, in salads or for dessert. Try other types of nuts, as well.

Linda Rosensteel **Sultana HS, Hesperia, CA**

Swedish Nuts

Makes a very large batch

3/4 cup butter
2 egg whites
pinch of salt
1 cup granulated sugar
1 large can salted mixed nuts

Preheat oven to 325 degrees. Melt the butter on a jelly roll pan. Beat the egg whites and salt with an electric mixer until the egg whites are stiff. Gradually add in the sugar while beating. The mixture will be grainy. Fold in the nuts. Spread onto the jelly roll pan. Bake for 30 minutes, turning the nuts every 10 minutes. Leave on the cookie sheet until cooled. Break apart.

This is a family recipe from my grandmother and mother. We make it every year for the holidays. We love it while watching the bowl games!

Deanna Lee **Marina HS, Huntington Beach, CA**

Cheesecakes

Butterscotch Dessert

Serves 12-16

Crust:
1 1/2 cups flour
1/2 cup margarine or butter
1/2 cup nuts, chopped
Cream Layer:
1/2 cup powdered sugar
8 ounces cream cheese
1 (9 ounces) carton Cool Whip
1/4 cup milk
Pudding Layer:
1 package butterscotch pudding, not instant
1 package coconut cream pudding, not instant
3 cups milk
1 (9 ounces) carton of Cool Whip, for topping

Preheat oven to 350 degrees. *Crust:* Cut first three ingredients together like pie crust. Pat in the bottom of a 9 x 13 cake pan. Bake for 15 minutes and cool. *Cream layer:* Mix together the powdered sugar, cream cheese, 1 carton Cool Whip, and 1/4 cup milk. Blend thoroughly and spread on cooled crust. *Pudding layer:* Mix butterscotch and coconut cream puddings together and cook, using 3 cups milk. Cool and spread over cream layer. Top with a carton of Cool Whip.

You will get compliments for this one. Everyone will want the recipe!

Linda A. Stokes **Riverton HS, Riverton, UT**

Cheesecake Parfait

Serves 6-12

1 package graham crackers, about 8
2 tablespoons sugar
3 tablespoons butter, melted
2 envelopes dream whip
1 cup cold milk
1 teaspoon vanilla
1(8 ounce) package cream cheese, softened
1 cup powdered sugar
fruit filling of your choice

Preheat oven to 375 degrees. Crush the graham crackers; add the sugar and melted butter; mix thoroughly. Spread out on an ungreased baking sheet. Bake for 10-15 minutes or until just toasted. Cool and crumble into a bowl. With an electric mixer whip the dream whip, milk and vanilla, until soft peaks form. In a separate bowl beat the cream cheese and powdered sugar; mix until smooth. Add the dream whip mixture and mix until smooth. To assemble parfaits, put a layer of graham cracker crumb mixture in a clear glass. Add a layer of cream filling, top with a layer of fruit filling. Repeat the layering until you have the desired size. To help with the layering I usually put the cream filling in a decorating bag, with or without a large tip. You can also add some chocolate syrup to the cream filling for a chocolate cheese cake, and use chocolate graham crackers for the crust.

This satisfies a cheese cake craving without much time or effort.
It also is a nice presentation for dinner parties and can be made ahead.

Shauna Young — Jordan HS, Sandy, UT

Chocolate Cheese Pie

Serves 6-8

1 cup evaporated milk, undiluted, divided
1 cup semisweet chocolate chips
2 egg yolks
1/3 cup sugar
1 (8 ounce) package soft cream cheese, cut into 1" pieces
1 9 inch graham cracker crumb crust
whipped cream

Pour 1/2 cup of the milk in ice cube tray; place in freezer until ice crystals form around edges. Heat remaining 1/2 cup of milk. Put chocolate chips and hot milk into a blender container; cover and process until smooth. Remove feeder cap and add egg yolks, one at a time, processing a few seconds after each addition. Add sugar, then add cream cheese pieces, one at a time, processing a few seconds after each addition. After last piece of cheese has been added, pour in the chilled milk and process until smooth and creamy. Pour into pie shell; cover and refrigerate until firm. Garnish with whipped cream and a few chocolate chips.

Smooth, rich and chocolatey!

Liz Aschenbrenner — Sierra HS, Manteca, CA

Karla's Cheesecake

Serves 6-8

Crust:
1 1/4 cups graham cracker crumbs (about 16)
1/4 cup sugar
1/2 cup melted butter
Cheese Cake Filling:
2 eggs
1/2 cup sugar
1 (8 ounce) package cream cheese , softened
1 teaspoon vanilla
cinnamon, (optional)

Preheat oven to 300 degrees. *Crust:* Combine crumbs and sugar. Add melted butter; stir to coat all crumbs. Press crumbs onto bottom and sides of pie pan. *Cheese Cake Filling:* Beat eggs until thick and lemon colored. Add sugar, cream cheese and vanilla; beat until smooth. Pour over crumb mixture. Bake for 30 minutes or until center is set. Do not over bake. Optional, sprinkle top with cinnamon; cool.

My best friend and college roommate shared this recipe with me more than thirty years ago. It was a family favorite in her Montana ranch home. It is simple and turns out great. Enjoy with or without a topping.

April Rosendahl **Chino HS, Chino, CA**

S'More Cheesecake Bites

Serves 6-8

1 (8 ounce) package cream cheese, softened
1/4 cup sugar
1/2 teaspoon vanilla
1 egg
1 1/2 cups Hershey's dark chocolate chips
1/2 cup milk
1 1/2 to 2 cups mini marshmallows
1/4 to 1/2 cup sliced almonds (optional)
9 (4 ounce) mini graham cracker pie crust

Preheat oven to 350 degrees. Beat cream cheese, sugar, & vanilla with mixer on medium speed until well blended. Add egg and beat one to two minutes longer. Melt chocolate chips in a microwave safe bowl on high for ONE minute, then stir chips with a spoon until completely melted. If needed, heat chips only a FEW seconds more being careful not to burn the chocolate chips. Add the melted chocolate chips and milk to batter and stir well. Fold in the marshmallows and sliced almonds (if desired) into the batter. Fill mini graham cracker pie crust with mixture and BAKE 10 to 15 minutes or until the center is set. Cool 5 to 10 minutes and refrigerate several hours or overnight.

This is a great tasting cheesecake that everyone loves. Kudos to Ashlee & Daniel for all of their hard work!

Jannie Parks **Ramona HS, Riverside, CA**

Vanilla Wafer Miniature Cheese Cake

Makes 22

2 (8 ounce) packages cream cheese, softened to room temperature
1 teaspoon vanilla
2 eggs
3/4 cup sugar
2 cans pie filling, any flavor
1 box vanilla wafers
22 (2 1/2 -inch) foil muffin tins

Preheat oven to 350 degrees. In a bowl, mix cream cheese, eggs and vanilla. After ingredients are mixed well, add sugar a little at a time. Put muffin cups on cookie sheet. Place vanilla wafer, flat side up, in each cup. Spoon cheese mixture on top to cover vanilla wafer, almost 1/2 full. Bake for 15-17 minutes. Cool, then top with pie filling.

A delicious family favorite.

Cheryl Moyle **Olympus HS, Salt Lake City, UT**

Cookies

Almond & Sesame Cookies

Makes 4 dozen

1 cup vegetable shortening
3/4 cup sugar
1 egg
1/2 teaspoon vanilla extract
2 teaspoons almond extract
2 3/4 cups flour, sifted
1/8 teaspoon baking soda
Topping
1 egg, scrambled
sesame seeds
almond slices

Preheat oven to 350 degrees. In large bowl cream together shortening and sugar. Using electric mixer, blend in 1 egg, vanilla, and almond extract. Now, using a wooden spoon, stir in flour and baking soda. After dough is mixed well, shape into small rounds the size of a quarter; flatten slightly. Dip each cookie into a plate of scrambled egg, then sesame seeds, top with almond slices. Bake on ungreased cookie sheet for 10 minutes.

Christine Becker Paradise HS, Paradise, CA

Bongo Bars

Serves 12-16

3/4 cup margarine
2 cups brown sugar
2 3/4 cups flour
2 1/2 teaspoons baking powder
3 eggs
1 teaspoon vanilla
bag of milk chocolate chips

Preheat oven to 350 degrees. Melt margarine and pour over brown sugar; stir together. Add dry ingredients. Add eggs and vanilla. Mix until dry ingredients are just moistened then add chocolate chips. Press into a 9 x 13 pan and bake for 30 minutes. Serve warm with vanilla ice cream.

I received this recipe many years ago when I was student teaching. One of my middle school students did a demonstration for the class and this was the recipe she made. It has been a family favorite ever since.

Darla Barton McKay HS, Salem, OR

Cappuccino Cookies

Makes 4 dozen

1 cup (2 sticks) butter, softened
2 cups light brown sugar
1/2 cup granulated sugar
2 eggs
4 teaspoons vanilla extract
3 1/2 cups all-purpose flour
1 teaspoon baking soda
1 teaspoon baking powder
1 teaspoon salt
1 tablespoon expresso powder
1 (12 ounces) bag cappuccino chips

Preheat oven to 350 degrees. In large mixing bowl, cream butter and sugars till light and fluffy. Beat in eggs and vanilla. Stir in dry ingredients. Gently fold in chips. Drop by tablespoonful, 1 inch apart, onto cookie sheet. Bake 11 minutes or until crisp on the bottom. Remove the cookie sheet and let cookies cool about 3 minutes before transferring them to a wire rack.

These cookies are sinful!

Astrid Curfman Newcomb Academy, Long Beach, CA

Chocolate Biscotti

Makes 24 large cookies

2/3 cup whole almonds, toasted
1 2/3 cups all-purpose flour
1/3 cup cocoa powder, unsweetened
1 teaspoon baking soda
1/2 teaspoon salt
1 cup sugar
3 large eggs, divided
2 large egg yolks
1/2 teaspoon pure vanilla extract
1/2 teaspoon almond extract
1 teaspoon grated orange zest
1 cup semisweet mini chocolate chips

Preheat oven to 350 degrees. Coarsely chop the almonds; set aside. Combine the flour, cocoa powder, baking soda, and salt in a large mixing bowl. Stir in the sugar. Add 2 of the whole eggs, the egg yolks, vanilla, almond extract, and orange zest. Mix with an electric mixer on low speed until just combined. Stir in the coarsely chopped almonds and mini chips. On a lightly floured surface divide the dough in half. Shape each half into a log 12 inches by 2 inches. Place the logs 2 inches apart on a greased or parchment lined cookie sheet. Beat the remaining whole egg and brush over the logs. Bake 35 minutes. They should be firm to touch. When cooled, transfer to a cutting board and cut into 1 inch slices. Preheat the oven to 325 degrees. Lay the slices cut side down on the baking sheet and return the cookies to the oven and bake another 10 minutes. Cool on wire racks.

Delicious biscotti with a twist.

Chrisann Boone — **Reedley HS, Reedley, CA**

Chocolate Mint M&M Cookies

Makes 2 dozen

1/2 cup butter, softened
1/2 cup brown sugar, packed
1/2 cup sugar
1 teaspoon vanilla
1/2 teaspoon salt
1/3 cup unsweetened cocoa powder
1 egg
1/2 teaspoon baking soda
1 cup all purpose flour
2 cups mint M & M's

Combine butter, brown sugar, sugar, vanilla, and salt; beat until light and fluffy. Add cocoa, egg and baking soda; mix until well blended. Stir in flour. Stir in M & M's. Chill dough 4-10 hours. Preheat oven to 325 degrees. Grease baking sheets; shape heaping tablespoons into balls. Bake 12-14 minutes. Cookies will be soft.

Mint M & M's are only available November and December. These cookies also freeze great and can be eaten later in the year.

Joyce Gifford **Desert Ridge HS, Mesa, AZ**

Chocolate-Glazed Shortbread

Makes 4 1/2 dozen

Cookies:
2 cups flour
1 cup quick oats, uncooked
3/4 teaspoon salt
1 cup butter, softened
1 cup confectioners' sugar
2 teaspoons vanilla
Chocolate Glaze:
1 cup semisweet chocolate chips
1 teaspoon vanilla
Decoration:
1 cup finely chopped nuts,
nonpareils, or colored sugar

Preheat oven to 325 degrees. In a small bowl, combine flour, oats and salt; set aside. In a large bowl, combine butter, confectioners' sugar and vanilla extract; beat until creamy. Gradually blend in flour mixture. Shape into 2 inch logs, using 1 rounded measuring teaspoon of dough for each cookie. Place on ungreased cookie sheets. Bake 20 -25 minutes. Let cool on cookie sheet 1 minute. Remove from cookie sheets; cool completely. Dip ends of cookies into Chocolate Glaze, then roll in the decoration of your choice. Chocolate Glaze: Over hot water, combine chocolate and vegetable shortening; stir until chips melt and the mixture is smooth.

Great shortbread. The oats add a wonderful flavor and texture. A real treat!

Laura May **Royal Oak Intermediate School, Covina, CA**

Cinnamon-Peanut Butter Cookies

Makes 3 dozen

1/2 cup butter
1/2 cup brown sugar
1/2 cup sugar
1/2 cup creamy peanut butter
1 egg
1 teaspoon vanilla
1 cup flour
1/2 teaspoon salt
1 teaspoon cinnamon

Preheat oven to 350 degrees. Beat together butter, sugars, peanut butter, egg and vanilla until well blended. Mix in flour, salt and cinnamon. Drop by heaping teaspoon on ungreased cookie sheet. Bake for 10-12 minutes or just until lightly golden.

Barbara Correia — Foothill HS, Pleasanton, CA

Cookies & Mallow bars

Serves 12-16

35 Chips Ahoy chocolate chip cookies, divided
1/3 cup margarine or butter, melted
15 ounces jet puffed marshmallow creme
1/3 cup Planters cocktail peanuts, chopped

Preheat oven to 350 degrees. Coarsely chop 15 cookies and set aside. Crush the remaining 20 cookies and mix with the margarine or butter. Press crumb mixture firmly into the bottom of a 9 x 13 inch greased pan. Top crust evenly with dollops of marshmallow creme and spread all the way to the edge. Top with the peanuts and reserved cookies. Bake 15 minutes or until marshmallow just begins to brown. Cool completely and cut into bars.

So easy and simple and takes no time.

Christine Rodriguez — Apple Valley HS, Apple Valley, CA

Cranberry Coconut Chews

Makes about 6 dozen

1 1/2 cups (3/4 pound) butter or margarine, room temperature
2 cups sugar
1 tablespoon orange peel, grated
2 teaspoons vanilla
3 1/4 cups all-purpose flour
1 teaspoon baking powder
1/4 teaspoon salt
1 1/2 cups dried cranberries
1 1/2 cups sweetened, flaked, dried coconut

Preheat oven to 350 degrees. In a large bowl, with a mixer on medium speed, beat butter, sugar, orange peel, and vanilla until smooth. In a medium bowl, mix flour, baking powder, and salt. Add to butter mixture. Beat on low speed until dough comes together, about 5 minutes. Mix in cranberries and coconut. (If the the batter seems slightly dry, that is OK and quite normal.) Shape dough into 1 inch balls and place about 2 inches apart on greased baking sheets. Bake in a 350 degree regular or convection oven until cookie edges just begin to brown, 8 to 11 minutes (shorter baking time will yield a chewier cookie; longer baking time will yield a crispier cookie). If baking two sheets at once in one oven, switch their positions halfway through baking. Let cookies cool on sheets for 5 minutes, then use a wide spatula to transfer to racks to cool completely.

Even if you don't like coconut, you'll love these cookies! They are a favorite of students and staff. My classes typically make them for the holiday season, and people always ask for the recipe. These cookies also freeze very well.

Tanya Trump — Eureka HS, Eureka, CA

Dad's Snickerdoodles

Makes 24-36

3/4 cup plus 2 tablespoons granulated sugar, divided
2 teaspoons ground cinnamon
1/2 cup butter or margarine
1 egg
1/2 teaspoon vanilla
1 1/2 cups flour
1/4 teaspoon salt
1/4 teaspoon baking soda
1/4 teaspoon cream of tartar

Combine 2 tablespoons sugar and cinnamon in a small bowl; then set aside. Cream butter and 3/4 cup sugar; add egg and vanilla. Mix dry ingredients together and add to butter mixture. Dough should be slightly sticky. Chill dough for 1-2 hours. Preheat oven to 375 degrees. Form into 1 inch balls and roll in cinnamon and sugar. Place on a greased baking sheet, and slightly flatten with the base of a cup or with a fork and leave the tine marks. Bake for 8-10 minutes. Cool and serve.

These can also be made without chilling.

Nancy Ball **Arbor View HS, Las Vegas, NV**

Easy Chocolate Covered Coconut Macaroons

Makes 2 dozen

3 1/3 cups flaked coconut
2/3 cup all purpose flour
1/8 teaspoon salt
1 (14 ounce) can sweetened condensed milk
1 1/4 teaspoons vanilla extract
1/2 cup semisweet chocolate chips

Preheat oven to 350 degrees. Grease cookie sheets. In a large bowl, stir together the coconut, flour and salt. Stir in the sweetened condensed milk and vanilla until everything is well blended. Drop by heaping spoonfuls onto the prepared pan. Bake for 12 to 15 minutes in the preheated oven, until coconut is sufficiently toasted. Immediately remove from cookie sheets to cool on wire racks. In the microwave or in a double boiler, melt chocolate chips stirring frequently until smooth; remove from heat and set aside to slightly cool. Then take a fork and drizzle chocolate on your freshly baked macaroons. Place onto waxed paper until chocolate has set.

These are so EASY and do not last long.
Double the recipe so you have some for later!

Alan von der Mehden **Pleasant Valley HS, Chico, CA**

Ginger Cookies

Makes about 30

3/4 cup shortening
1 cup sugar
1 egg
4 tablespoons molasses
2 cups flour
1 teaspoon cinnamon
1 teaspoon ground ginger
1 teaspoon ground cloves
2 teaspoons baking soda

Preheat oven to 375 degrees. Mix all ingredients together thoroughly. Roll into small 1" balls. Dip each ball into sugar and press down onto baking sheet with the bottom of a glass. Bake for 10 minutes.

This is my son's all time favorite cookie. A soft version of a "gingersnap".

Adriana Molinaro **Granite Hills HS, El Cajon, CA**

Gingerbread Men

Makes 2 dozen

1 (3.5 ounce) package cook and serve butterscotch pudding
1/2 cup butter
1/2 cup brown sugar
1 egg
1 1/2 cups all-purpose flour
1/2 teaspoon baking soda
1 1/2 teaspoons ground ginger
1 teaspoon ground cinnamon

In large bowl, use an electric mixer and cream together dry pudding mix, butter, and brown sugar. Add egg and beat thoroughly. In medium bowl, combine flour, baking soda, ginger and cinnamon. Add to butter mixture and blend until a soft dough forms. Use your hands to shape dough into 2 or 3 balls. Place dough balls into a baggy and refrigerate at least 1 hour. Preheat oven to 350 degrees. Roll out dough on a floured counter to 1/8 inch thickness. Cut with cookie cutter. Place 2 inches apart on a greased baking sheet. Bake for 10-12 minutes or until cookies are golden at the edges.

My students love these cookies. A great lab for the holidays.

Carol Steele **Arroyo Seco JHS, Valencia, CA**

Hawaiian Cookie Tarts

Makes 3 dozen

1 3/4 cups flour
1/2 cup powdered sugar
2 tablespoons cornstarch
1 cup butter, softened
1 teaspoon vanilla
Filling:
1 cup pineapple preserves
1/2 cup sugar
1 egg
1 1/2 cups coconut
powdered sugar

Heat oven to 350 degrees. In large bowl, combine flour, powdered sugar and cornstarch; blend well. Add butter and vanilla. By hand, blend until soft dough forms. Shape dough into 1 inch balls. Place 1 ball in each of 36 ungreased miniature muffin cups; press in bottom and up sides of each cup. Spoon 1 teaspoon of the pineapple preserves into each dough-lined cup. In small bowl, combine sugar and egg. Using fork, beat until well blended. Stir in coconut until well coated with egg mixture. Spoon 1 teaspoonful coconut mixture over pineapple preserves in each cup. Bake for 23 -33 minutes or until crusts are very light golden brown. Cool 20 minutes. To release cookies from cups, hold muffin pan upside down at an angle over wire rack. Using handle of table knife, firmly tap bottom each cup until cookie releases. Cool completely. Just before serving sprinkle with powdered sugar.

Every time we make these cookies in the restaurant they are sold out. They are also great for party trays.

Karen Tilson **Poly HS, Riverside, CA**

Lemon Bars

Makes 12-16

Crust:
1 cup butter
2 cups flour
1/2 cup powdered sugar
Filling:
4 eggs, beaten
2 cups granulated sugar
1/3 cup fresh lemon juice
1 tablespoon grated lemon zest
1/2 teaspoon baking powder
1/4 cup flour

Preheat oven to 350 degrees. Cut butter into flour and powdered sugar until crumbly. Pat into a 9 x 13 pan and bake for 25 minutes. Combine filling ingredients together and pour over baked crust. Return to oven and continue to bake an additional 20-25 minutes. Dust with powdered sugar when cooled.

I make these lemon bars with the lemons from my tree.
These delicious bars are always a hit!

Adriana Molinaro **Granite Hills HS, El Cajon, CA**

Lemon Cookies

Makes 3 dozen

6 ounces unsalted butter
1 1/2 cups sugar
1 egg
1 tablespoon lemon juice
2 tablespoons milk
1 teaspoon vanilla extract
3 1/2 cups all-purpose flour
2 teaspoons baking powder
1/2 teaspoon salt

Preheat oven to 350 degrees. Cream unsalted butter and sugar until light yellow. Beat in egg. Add lemon juice, milk and vanilla. Sift together flour, baking powder and salt. Mix the dry ingredients into the butter mixture and blend well. You may have to knead in the last part of the flour. Form dough into 1 inch diameter balls by rolling dough between your hands. Lightly roll in flour and place 3 inches apart on a buttered cookie sheet. Press the patterned surface of a cookie stamp into flour and shake off excess, then press the balls of dough flat. Bake 10-12 minutes until golden on the edges.

A delicious accompaniment to an afternoon tea.

Lisa Burson **San Luis Obispo HS, San Luis Obispo, CA**

My Favorite Lemon Squares

Makes 24 squares

1 cup butter
2 cups plus 4 tablespoons flour, divided
1/2 cup confectioners' sugar
4 eggs
4 tablespoons lemon juice
2 cups granulated sugar
1 teaspoon baking powder
1/2 teaspoon salt
additional confectioners' sugar

Preheat oven to 350 degrees. Melt butter in a 13 x 9 x 2 inch baking pan. Add 2 cups flour and 1/2 cup confectioners' sugar; mix. Pat down flat in pan. Bake for 20 minutes. Meanwhile, in a medium mixing bowl, beat eggs and lemon juice until light. Sift together remaining 4 tablespoons flour, granulated sugar, baking powder, and salt. Add to egg mixture. Mix well. Pour over hot crust. Return to oven and bake 25 minutes. Sift confectioners' sugar over top. Cool. Cut into 24 squares.

Pam Ford **Temecula Valley HS, Temecula, CA**

Oatmeal Crispies

Makes 24

1/4 cup shortening
1/4 cup margarine or butter
1/2 cup sugar
1/2 cup brown sugar
1 egg
1/2 teaspoon vanilla
3/4 cup flour, unsifted
1/2 teaspoon baking soda
1/2 teaspoon salt
1 1/2 cups oatmeal
1/4 cup walnuts, finely chopped

Preheat oven to 350 degrees. Beat together first 6 ingredients until light and creamy. Sift together the flour, soda and salt. Add to the butter mixture and blend together. Stir in the oatmeal and the walnuts. Drop onto a greased cookie sheet, leaving room for expansion. Bake for 8 minutes.

These are the best oatmeal cookies I have ever eaten. They are crisp and chewy. My students love them!

Diane Lizardi **Downey HS, Downey, CA**

Peanut Butter Chocolate Bars

Makes 24 bars

1 yellow cake mix
1 cup smooth peanut butter
1 cube butter, melted
2 eggs
Filling:
1 (12 ounce) package semisweet chocolate chips
1 (14 ounce) can sweetened condensed milk
2 tablespoons butter
2 teaspoons vanilla

Preheat oven to 325 degrees and set aside an ungreased 9 x 13 pan. Put cake mix, peanut butter, melted butter and eggs in large mixing bowl. Blend with electric mixer on low for 1 minute or until combined. Reserve 1 1/2 cups of mixture for topping. Put remaining mixture in 9 x 13 pan and use fingertips to press the crust evenly over the bottom of the pan until it reaches all sides. For the filling: put chocolate chips, sweetened condensed milk and butter in a large saucepan. Place over low heat and stir and cook until chocolate is melted and mixture is well combined, 3-4 minutes. Remove from heat and add vanilla. Pour chocolate mixture over crust and spread evenly. Crumble the reserved crust evenly over the chocolate. Bake for 20-25 minutes or until light brown. Cool and cut into 24 bars.

This is a delicious combination of chocolate and peanut butter.

Rebecca Zavala — Selma HS, Selma, CA

Persimmon Cookies

Makes 4 dozen

1/2 cup margarine
1/2 cup brown sugar
1/2 cup granulated sugar
1 egg
1 cup persimmon pulp, sieved
1/2 teaspoon cloves
1/2 teaspoon nutmeg
2 cups flour
1 teaspoon soda
1/2 teaspoon salt
1 teaspoon cinnamon
1 cup nuts, chopped
1 cup raisins or dates, optional

Preheat oven to 375 degrees. Cream margarine and sugars, add egg and mix well. Mix in pulp, then add dry ingredients which have been sifted together. Add nuts and raisins or dates, if desired. Drop by spoonfuls on greased cookie sheet. Bake for 10-12 minutes.

This cookie is a seasonal family favorite. It is very moist with a cake texture.

Patricia Perry — Willows HS, Willows, CA

Pumpkin Bars

Makes 50 bars

2 cups sugar
1/2 cup vegetable oil
1 (16 ounce) can pumpkin
4 eggs, beaten
2 cups Bisquick Baking Mix
2 teaspoons cinnamon
1/2 cup raisins
Cream Cheese Frosting:
1 (3 ounce) package cream cheese, softened
1/3 cup butter, softened
1 tablespoon milk
1 teaspoon vanilla
2 cups powdered sugar

Heat oven to 350 degrees. Grease jelly roll pan. Beat sugar, oil, pumpkin and eggs in large bowl on medium speed (scrape bowl occasionally) one minute. Stir in baking mix, cinnamon and raisins. Pour into pan. Bake 25-30 minutes. Cool. Frost with Cream Cheese Frosting. Cut into bars, 3 x 1 inch. Refrigerate. Beat cream cheese, butter, milk and vanilla until creamy. Stir in powdered sugar until smooth.

This recipe is moist and delicious. It makes a great gift tray.

Renee Paulsin **Hemet HS, Hemet, CA**

Pumpkin Dip for Ginger Snaps

Makes about 2 cups

1 cup powdered sugar
1 (8 ounce) block cream cheese
1/2 can (15 ounce) pumpkin
nutmeg, to taste
cinnamon, to taste

Cream sugar and cream cheese with a blender. Add pumpkin and spices until well blended. Serve with ginger snaps.

This was passed on by a great friend from Florida.
Perfect light dessert after a heavy holiday meal.

Dawn Maceyka **Great Oak HS, Temecula, CA**

Ranger Cookies

Makes 4 dozen

2 cups sugar
2 cups brown sugar
2 cups butter
4 eggs
4 teaspoons vanilla
5 cups flour
4 teaspoons baking soda
4 teaspoons baking powder
48 ounces chocolate chips
8 cups Honey Bunches of Oats with Almonds Cereal (Blue Box)
14 ounces coconut

Preheat oven to 375 degrees. Cream together sugar, brown sugar, butter, eggs, and vanilla. Stir together, then mix in flour, baking soda, and baking powder. Add chocolate chips, cereal, and coconut. Bake 8-10 minutes.

Shirley Marshman **West MS, Downey, CA**

Raspberry Bars

Makes 25 bars

1 1/2 cups butter (must be butter)
3 (12 ounce) bags white chocolate chips, divided
6 eggs
1 1/2 cups sugar
3 1/4 cups flour
1 1/2 teaspoons salt
3 teaspoons pure almond extract
2 cups raspberry jam
1 small bag (1/2 cup) toasted almonds

Heat oven to 325 degrees. Grease and flour large cookie sheet. Melt butter on low heat. Remove and add 1/2 of the white chocolate chips. Do not stir; let stand. Beat eggs until foamy. Gradually add sugar and stir into white chocolate mix. Stir in flour and salt. Add extract and mix. Spread 1/2 of the mixture onto cookie sheet. Bake 15-20 minutes, just until golden brown. Add remaining white chocolate chips into batter and stir. Let crust cool completely. When cooled, spread jam over crust. Spoon remaining batter on top of jam in spoonfuls and then spread. Sprinkle on toasted sliced almonds. Bake 20-25 minutes until golden brown. Let cool. Cut into squares.

Karma Bateman **Jordan HS, Sandy, UT**

Rocky Road Bars

Makes 24-30 bars

1 (12 ounce) bag semi sweet chocolate chips
1 (12 ounce) bag butterscotch chips
1/2 cup crunchy peanut butter
10 ounces mini marshmallows
1 cup peanuts

Melt the two bags of chocolate and butterscotch chips with peanut butter in a large microwave bowl for 1 minute. Stir and return to microwave for 1-2 more minutes. Cool for 3 minutes. Stir in marshmallows and peanuts to chocolate mixture. Pour into a buttered 9 x 13 pan. Cut when cool.

Easy and always a hit!

Sue Waterbury **San Luis Obispo HS, San Luis Obispo, CA**

S'More Cookie Bars

Makes 2 dozen

3/4 cup butter
3 cups graham cracker crumbs
1 cup semi sweet chocolate chips
1 cup butterscotch chips
1 cup mini marshmallows
1 can sweetened condensed milk

Preheat oven to 350 degrees. Place graham crackers in a large plastic bag, using a rolling pin make crumbs. Melt butter in the microwave for 40 seconds.

Combine butter and crackers and press into a 9 x 13 inch oven safe dish. Sprinkle chocolate chips, butterscotch chips, and marshmallows evenly over the crust. Bake 25 minutes or until bubbly. Cool for 15 minutes on wire rack. Place in refrigerator until cool. Cut and serve.

A rich dessert that came from my mom.

Kristi Melton **Marina HS, Huntington Beach, CA**

Snickers Surprise Cookies

Makes two dozen

2 sticks butter, softened
1 cup creamy peanut butter
1 cup light brown sugar
1 cup sugar
2 eggs
1 teaspoon vanilla
3 1/2 cups all purpose flour, sifted
1/2 teaspoon salt
1 teaspoon baking soda
1 (13 ounce) package Snickers Miniatures

Combine the butter, peanut butter, and sugars using a mixer on a medium to low speed until light and fluffy. Slowly add eggs and vanilla until thoroughly combined. Then mix in flour, salt and baking soda. Cover and chill dough for 2-3 hours. Unwrap all Snickers. Remove dough from refrigerator. Divide into 1 tablespoon pieces and flatten. Place a Snickers in the center of each piece of dough. Form the dough into a ball around each Snickers. Place on a greased cookie sheet and bake at 325 degrees for 10-12 minutes. Let cookies cool on baking rack or wax paper. Hint: Spruce up cookies by drizzling melted chocolate over the top of each cookie.

If you like peanut butter, you'll love these treats!

Laura Lewis **Garden Grove HS, Garden Grove, CA**

Something-for-Everyone Cookies

Makes 2 dozen 3-inch cookies

1 1/2 cups all-purpose flour
1 teaspoon baking soda
1 cup (2 sticks) unsalted butter, room temperature
3/4 cup granulated sugar
3/4 cup light-brown sugar
1 egg
1 teaspoon pure vanilla extract
1 1/2 cups oatmeal
1 cup dried cherries
1 cup bittersweet chocolate, coarsely chopped
1 cup (5 1/2 ounces) toffee pieces

Preheat oven to 350 degrees. Sift together flour and baking soda and set aside. In the bowl of an electric mixer fitted with the paddle attachment, cream butter and sugars on medium-high speed until light and fluffy, 2 to 3 minutes. Scrape down the sides of the bowl once or twice during mixing. Add egg and mix on high speed to combine. Add vanilla extract; mix to combine. Scrape down the sides of the bowl. Add the sifted flour a bit at a time on a low speed until well combined. Add oatmeal, cherries, chocolate, and toffee pieces; mix to combine. Divide dough into three equal portions, and roll into logs using plastic wrap, approximately 1 1/2 inches in diameter. To bake, cut logs into 3/4-inch pieces. Bake on parchment-lined baking sheets, until golden brown, 8 to 10 minutes. Remove from oven and transfer to a baking rack to cool.

I once heard Martha Stewart say these were her favorite cookies. This oatmeal-cookie dough can be baked immediately, refrigerated for one to two days, or frozen for up to a month.

Tisha Ludeman — **Brookhurst JHS, Anaheim, CA**

Tropical Peanut Squares

Makes 15

1 cup light corn syrup
1 cup brown sugar, firmly packed
1 cup peanut butter
6 cups Special K cereal
2 cups flaked coconut

Place corn syrup and brown sugar in saucepan. Cook over medium heat till mixture bubbles; remove from heat. Stir in peanut butter. Add Special K cereal and coconut. Stir until well coated. Spray 9 x 13 pan with Pam, then press mixture into pan. Cut into squares when cool.

A lot like Rice Crispie Treats with a tropical twist!!

Pam James — **Live Oak HS, Live Oak, CA**

Frozen Desserts

Eloise's Pink Frozen Salad

Serves 12

1 can Comstock Cherry Pie Filling
1 (20 ounce) can crushed pineapple, drained
1 can condensed milk
1 teaspoon almond flavoring
12 ounces Cool Whip

Mix together the first four ingredients. Fold in the Cool Whip. Place in 13 x 9 glass baking dish and freeze. Cut into squares and serve as a salad on lettuce or as a dessert.

Tennessee folks love this, and it keeps for a long time.

Sonja Shumaker — **Ruben S. Ayala HS, Chino Hills, CA**

German Chocolate Ice Cream

Makes 1 gallon

1 (4 ounce) bar German chocolate
2 cans evaporated milk
5-6 eggs
2 1/2 cups sugar
2 tablespoons vanilla
pinch of salt
1 pint half and half
whole milk

Melt chocolate bar and 1 can of milk in saucepan. Cool. Pour in blender and whip with eggs. Transfer to ice cream freezer can. In the blender whip second can of milk, sugar, vanilla, and salt. Add to ice cream freezer. Add half and half to freezer and then fill with whole milk to fill line on ice cream freezer. Follow directions on ice cream freezer to complete the process. Enjoy.

Yummy for summer parties and barbecues.

Kris Briney — **Fresno HS, Fresno, CA**

Ice Cream Sandwich Dessert

Serves 15

24-30 ice cream sandwiches
1 (20 ounce) container Cool Whip, divided
6 Health Bars, crushed, divided
hot fudge or caramel topping

Cover the bottom of a 9 x 13 dish with 12-15 ice cream sandwiches, fitting together tightly and cutting to achieve uniformity. Add a layer of 1/2 the Cool Whip frosted onto the ice cream sandwiches. Sprinkle 1/2 of the crushed candy bars on top of the Cool Whip. Repeat layers, topping with crumbled candy bars. Freeze until time to serve; drizzle with chocolate or caramel sauce individually.

Everyone is amazed with this dessert; they can't believe what it is and how easy. You can use peppermint candies (crushed) or other sauces.

Wendy Duncan **West Covina HS, West Covina, CA**

Soft Serve Ice Cream

Serves 1-2

1 cup half and half
2 tablespoons sugar
1 egg
1 teaspoon vanilla
1 quart ice
1/4-1/2 cup rock salt
1 small Zip-lock bag
1 large Zip-lock bag

Mix together the first 4 ingredients; place in small Zip-lock bag and seal. Place ice and rock salt in large bag; insert small bag into large bag and seal. Shake vigorously until you have "soft serve."

Fun for kids with easy clean up, too!

Joanne Montoy **Esperanza HS, Anaheim, CA**

Fruits, Cobblers, & Gelatins

Apple Marzipan Galette

Serves 8

$^1/_2$ (15 ounce) package refrigerated pie dough
(such as Pillsbury)
cooking spray
$^1/_2$ cup marzipan, softened
4 cups (about 2 pounds) Granny Smith apples, peeled, sliced
8 tablespoons sugar, divided
1 tablespoon all purpose flour
$^1/_2$ teaspoon almond extract, divided
2 teaspoons lemon juice
dash of salt

Preheat oven to 425 degrees. Line a jelly roll pan with foil; coat foil with cooking spray. Roll dough to a 14 inch circle on a lightly floured surface. Place dough on a prepared pan. Roll marzipan to a 9 inch circle on a lightly floured surface. Place marzipan on top of dough. Combine apples, 2 tablespoons sugar, flour, $^1/_4$ teaspoon almond extract, lemon juice and salt in a large bowl; toss well. Spoon apple mixture over marzipan. Fold 2 inch dough border over the apple mixture, pressing gently to seal (dough will only partially cover apple mixture). Bake for 30 minutes or until lightly browned (apple filling may leak slightly during cooking). Place remaining 6 tablespoons sugar in a small, heavy saucepan over medium-high heat; cook until sugar dissolves, stirring as needed to dissolve the sugar evenly (about 4 minutes). Cook 1 minute or until golden. Remove from heat; carefully stir in $^1/_4$ teaspoon almond extract. Drizzle over galette.

Michele Casale — **San Mateo HS, San Mateo, CA**

Apple-Cranberry Crisp

Serves 10-12

6 cups apples, peeled and thinly sliced
(about 6 medium apples, preferably Granny Smith)
1/2 cup fresh or frozen cranberries, rinsed
1 1/3 cups quick or old-fashioned oats, uncooked
1/2 cup all purpose flour
1/2 cup light brown sugar, packed
1/2 teaspoon cinnamon
1/4 teaspoon ground ginger
1/4 teaspoon salt
dash ground nutmeg
1/4 cup (1/2 stick) cold butter, cut into pieces

Grease the inside of a medium (4-6 quart) crock-pot stoneware with butter or Pam for Baking. Mix together the prepared apples and cranberries in the prepared stoneware. Combine oats, flour, brown sugar, cinnamon, ginger, salt , and nutmeg in a medium bowl. Cut in butter with pastry blender or two knives until mixture resembles coarse crumbs. Sprinkle oats mixture over apple mixture; smooth top. Cover, cook on LOW for about 4 hours or on HIGH for about 2 hours, or until apples are tender. Serve either topped with whipped cream or over vanilla ice cream.

I adapted this recipe from one provided by Rival Crock Pot. It's easy, tastes great, and keeps your oven free for other baking during the holidays.

Ellen Gordon — **Colton HS, Colton, CA**

Berry Parfait with Apricot Zabaione (Italian Custard)

Serves 4-6

5 egg yolks
1 egg
2 tablespoons sugar
1/2 cup apricot nectar
2 cups mixed fresh berries

Combine the egg yolks, egg and sugar in the top of a double boiler set above simmering water. Beat the mixture with a wire whisk or a rotary beater until it is pale yellow and fluffy. (A portable electric mixer makes this job much easier) Gradually add the apricot nectar and continue beating until the Zabaione becomes thick enough to hold is shape in a spoon. The process can take as long as 10 minutes or more. Layer the Zabaione with the fresh berries in parfait glasses and chill until served.

This recipe is originally made with Marsala, but the apricot nectar makes a wonderful nonalcoholic alternative. The parfait may also be served warm.

Pamela Bonilla — **Valley View HS, Moreno Valley, CA**

Do-Not-Stir Cobbler

Serves 6-8

1/2 cup butter
1 cup sugar
1 cup flour
dash salt
2 teaspoons baking powder
2/3 cup milk
2 cups fruit with juice (peaches)
1/4 cup sugar for topping

Preheat oven to 350 degrees. Melt butter in a casserole dish. Make batter of sugar, flour, salt, baking powder, and milk. Pour batter into butter in casserole but do not stir. Pour fruit with juice, such as canned peaches, over batter; do not stir. Sprinkle sugar on top. Do not stir. Bake for 45 minutes. Serve warm with whipped cream or ice cream.

This recipe is one of our family traditions!

Cheryl Whittington — **Saddleback HS, Santa Ana, CA**

Fresh Fruit & Nut Parfait

Serves 8

1 cup pineapple, cut into bite sized chunks
1 cup strawberries
1 orange, peeled and sectioned
3 kiwifruit, peeled and sliced
1 cup blueberries
1 teaspoon lemon juice
8 ounces light cream cheese, room temperature
1/3 cup sugar
1/2 teaspoon vanilla
8 tablespoons peanuts, chopped

Combine fruit and toss with lemon juice. In a small bowl, combine cream cheese, sugar, and vanilla. Whip with an electric mixer on medium speed, until light and fluffy. Divide fruit into 8 glasses. Top with cream cheese and sprinkle with nuts.

Fanua Matagi — **Chino HS, Chino, CA**

Jackfruit Salad-Vietnamese

Serves 18

1 cup walnuts, coarsely chopped
6 cups Jackfruit, diced
2 cups jicama, diced
1 lime, juiced
1 cup coconut
3/4 cup golden raisins
2 cups sour cream

Toast walnuts on a cookie sheet at 300 degrees for 8-10 minutes, turning once; set aside. Combine all ingredients except toasted walnuts in a large bowl. Stir well. Add the toasted walnuts just before serving and stir well.

Maria Nicholaides **Oceanview HS, Huntington Beach, CA**

Lil's Pecan Pumpkin Crumble

Serves 12

1 cup sugar
1 1/2 teaspoons pumpkin pie spice
2 eggs
1 (16 ounce) can pumpkin
1 (12 ounce) can evaporated milk
1/2 box yellow cake mix
1/2 cup margarine
3/4 cup pecans, chopped
whipping cream

Preheat oven to 350 degrees. Mix together the first 5 ingredients. Pour into an ungreased 9 x 13 glass pan. Sprinkle the cake mix over the pumpkin mixture. Melt the margarine and drizzle over the cake mix. Sprinkle the pecans on top. Bake for 40-45 minutes. Cool and serve with whipping cream.

A new addition to a Thanksgiving meal.

Sonja Shumaker **Ruben S Ayala HS, Chino Hills, CA**

Old Fashioned Apple Crisp

Serves 6-8

Filling:
5 pounds Macintosh, Golden Delicious, or Gala apples
2 tablespoons orange juice, freshly squeezed
2 tablespoons lemon juice, freshly squeezed
1/2 cup granulated sugar
2 teaspoons ground cinnamon
1 teaspoon ground nutmeg
Topping:
1 1/2 cups flour
3/4 cup granulated sugar
3/4 cup light brown sugar, packed
1/2 teaspoon kosher salt
1 cup oatmeal, old fashioned
1/2 pound cold unsalted butter, diced

Preheat the oven to 350 degrees. Butter a 9 x 14 by 2 inch oval baking dish. Peel, core, and cut the apples into large wedges. Combine the apples with the juices, sugar, and spices. Pour into the dish. To make the topping, combine the flour, sugars, salt, oatmeal, and cold butter in the bowl of an electric mixer fitted with the paddle attachment. Mix on low speed until the mixture is crumbly and the butter is the size of peas. Scatter evenly over the apples. Place the baking dish on a sheet pan to catch any filling that bubbles over and bake for 1 hour or until the top is brown and the fruit filling bubbles. Serve warm.

In a hurry? Use prepared Comstock's Cherry Pie Filling in place of the apple filling.

Pat Doler **Ventura HS, Ventura, CA**

Pear & Apple Crisp

Serves 12-16

4-5 pears
4-5 apples
2 tablespoons lemon juice
1/2 cup dried berries or raisins
6 tablespoons margarine
2/3 cup all-purpose flour
2/3 cup rolled oats
2/3 cup brown sugar
1 teaspoon cinnamon
1/2 teaspoon allspice or nutmeg
vanilla ice cream or nonfat frozen yogurt (optional)

Heat oven to 375 degrees. Lightly grease a baking pan. Core and slice pears and apples; toss with lemon juice in the large metal bowl. Arrange pears, apples and dried fruit in a 9 x 13 inch baking dish. In a medium-large bowl, mix margarine & flour; cut in with a pastry blender until mixture looks crumbly. Mix oats into margarine & flour mixture using a wooden spoon. Add brown sugar & spices to topping mixture; mix well with wooden spoon. Sprinkle mixture evenly over fruit and press down lightly. Bake 20 to 25 minutes until pears and apples are tender. Serve warm with ice cream

I was inspired to create this recipe after receiving a donation of home grown pears from Kenilworths' most spirited math teacher, Mrs. Ayotte.
It is a fabulous, tasty dessert.

Alicia Pucci **Kenilworth JHS, Petaluma, CA**

Raspberry Angel Cake Dessert

Serves 10-12

1 (6 ounce) package raspberry Jell-O
1 1/4 cups boiling water
1 (10 ounce) package frozen raspberries
1 cup whipping cream, whipped
1 angel food cake

Dissolve Jell-O in water: add berries and stir until they thaw. Chill until partially set, then whip until fluffy. Fold in whipped cream. Break cake into pieces, and mix them into the Jell-O mixture. Spread in 9 x 13 pan. Chill overnight.

Another way to enjoy my favorite fruit!

Gaylen Roe **Magnolia JHS, Chino, CA**

Raspberry Pretzel Dessert

Serves 8-12

2 cups pretzels, crushed
1 cup butter, melted
1 cup plus 2 tablespoons powdered sugar, divided
11 ounces cream cheese, softened
12 ounces Cool Whip
2 large packages raspberry Jell-O
4 cups boiling water
2 packages frozen raspberries, partially thawed

Preheat oven to 350 degrees. Mix pretzels, butter, and 2 tablespoons powdered sugar. Press into a 9 x 13 deep pan. Bake 15 minutes. Cool. Whip cream cheese, Cool Whip and 1 cup powdered sugar until smooth. Spread over pretzel crust, making sure to seal to edge of pan. Combine Jell-O and boiling water and stir until Jell-O is dissolved. Stir in raspberries. Pour over Cool Whip layer. Chill at least 2 hours before serving.

This recipe was passed to me by my stepdaughter, Stacy. She had made changes to the recipe she liked, and I have made changes that I like!

Suzi Schneider **Bret Harte HS, Angels Camp, CA**

Pies & Pastries

Apple Bistro Tart

Serves 8

1 unbaked pie crust
1 tablespoon sugar
1 teaspoon ground cinnamon
1/4 teaspoon ground ginger
1/8 teaspoon nutmeg
1 teaspoon lemon peel, finely shredded
2-3 medium tart green apples, peeled, cored, and cut into 1/4 inch thick slices
1/2 cup caramel apple dip
1/2 cup pecans, coarsely chopped
1/4 cup apple jelly
powdered sugar

Preheat oven to 425 degrees. Let pie crust stand according to package directions. Meanwhile, in a medium bowl combine sugar, cinnamon, ginger, nutmeg, and lemon peel. Add apple slices and toss to coat. Place unfolded pie crust on a large cookie sheet. Spread caramel apple dip over crust to within 2 inches of edges. Place apple mixture over caramel. Sprinkle with pecans. Fold sides of crust about 2 inches up and over apples, folding edges as necessary. Bake for 20 minutes or until crust is golden brown and apples are just tender (tent with foil if pecans start darkening before the tart is done). Meanwhile, in a small saucepan melt apple jelly over low heat. Remove tart from oven and brush melted jelly over entire tart, including pastry. Serve warm. Sift powdered sugar over tart before serving.

This recipe was modified from a prize-winning recipe in Better Homes and Gardens *magazine. Great served warm with ice cream.*

Millie Deeton — **Ruben S. Ayala HS, Chino Hills, CA**

Buttermilk Pie

Serves 6-8

4 eggs
1 cup buttermilk
1/3 cup butter, melted
1 teaspoon vanilla
1 1/4 cups sugar
2 tablespoons flour
1 pinch salt
1 pinch nutmeg, freshly ground
1 unbaked 9-inch pie crust

Preheat oven to 400 degrees. In a large mixing bowl beat eggs and buttermilk. Melt butter in a separate bowl and add to mixture. Add all other ingredients and mix thoroughly. Pour filling into a prepared, uncooked 9 inch pie shell. Bake at 400 degrees for 10 minutes, lower temperature to 350 degrees and continue cooking for 50-60 minutes. Remove pie from oven when only the very center jiggles a little. Cool to room temperature. Serve with fresh berries and whipped cream.

After experimenting with every recipe out there, this one is finally the perfect balance of sweet and creamy. Everyone loves it!

Camille Williams — **Provo HS, Provo, UT**

Caramel Nut Tart

Serves 6-8

1/2 cup heavy whipping cream
2 tablespoons instant coffee
1 (14 ounce) bag of caramels
4 cups pecans or almonds, toasted
1/4 teaspoon cinnamon
1 graham cracker crust
1/2 cup chocolate chips

Special Dark Chocolate Chip Scones

Makes 24

3 1/4 cups all-purpose flour
1/2 cup sugar
1 tablespoon plus 1 teaspoon baking powder
1/4 teaspoon salt
2 cups (12-oz. pkg.) Hershey's Special Dark Chocolate Chips
1/2 cup chopped nuts(optional)
2 cups chilled whipping cream
2 tablespoons butter, melted
Additional sugar
Powdered sugar(optional)

Heat oven to 375 F. Lightly grease 2 baking sheets. Stir together flour, 1/2 cup sugar, baking powder and salt in large bowl. Stir in chocolate chips and nuts, if desired. Stir whipping cream into flour mixture, stirring just until ingredients are moistened. Turn mixture out onto lightly floured surface. Knead gently until soft dough forms (about 2 minutes). Divide dough into three equal balls. One ball at a time, flatten into 7-inch circle; cut into 8 triangles. Transfer triangles to prepared baking sheets, spacing 2 inches apart. Brush with melted butter and sprinkle with additional sugar. Bake 15 to 20 minutes or until lightly browned. Serve warm, sprinkled with powdered sugar, if desired. 24 scones.

Recipes and photos courtesy of Hershey's Kitchens

Chocolate & Peanut Butter Truffles

Makes 3 1/2 dozen

3/4 cup (1 1/2 sticks) butter (no substitutes)
1 cup Reese's Peanut Butter Chips
1/2 cup Hershey's Cocoa
1 can (14 oz.) sweetened condensed milk (not evaporated milk)
1 tablespoon vanilla extract
Hershey's Cocoa or finely chopped nuts or graham cracker crumbs

Melt butter and peanut butter chips in large saucepan over very low heat, stirring often. Add cocoa; stir until smooth. Stir in sweetened condensed milk; stir constantly about 4 minutes or until mixture is thick and glossy. Remove from heat; stir in vanilla. Refrigerate 2 hours or until firm enough to handle. Shape into 1-inch balls; roll in cocoa, nuts or graham cracker crumbs. Refrigerate until firm, about 1 hour. Store, covered, in refrigerator.

Special Dark Chocolate Chip Scones

Chocolate & Peanut Butter Truffles

Easy Berry Mousse

Peach Crisp

Easy Berry Mousse

Serves 8

1 cup boiling water
1 pkg. (4-serving size) strawberry gelatin
2 extra-ripe, medium Dole Bananas
1 carton (8 oz.) strawberry yogurt
2 cups frozen non-dairy whipped topping, thawed
1 cup Dole Fresh Frozen Whole Strawberries or Mixed Berries, thawed, sliced and drained
Dole Strawberry Slices (optional)

Stir boiling water into gelatin in medium bowl at least 2 minutes until completely dissolved. Place in freezer about 20 minutes, stirring occasionally or until slightly thickened. Puree bananas in blender or food processor container (1 cup.) Combine yogurt and pureed bananas in large bowl. Blend gelatin mixture into banana mixture. Refrigerate until slightly thickened. Fold whipped topping into gelatin mixture with sliced strawberries. Spoon gelatin mixture into serving bowl. Refrigerate until firm. Garnish with additional strawberries, if desired.

Recipes and photos courtesy of Dole Foods

Peach Crisp

Serves 6

1 1/4 cups all-purpose flour, divided
1 cup packed brown sugar, divided
1/4 teaspoon salt
1/2 cup plus 5 tablespoons butter or margarine, divided
2 bags (16 oz. each) Dole Fresh-Frozen Sliced Peaches, thawed
1/2 cup granulated sugar
1/4 cup cornstarch
1 1/2 cups rolled oats

Combine 1 cup flour, 1/2 cup brown sugar and salt in medium bowl. Cut in 1/2 cup butter until crumbly. Pat into bottom of greased 9-inch square baking dish. Bake at 350°F., 15 minutes. Combine granulated sugar and cornstarch; stir in peaches. Pour into crust. Combine oats, remaining 1/2 cup brown sugar and 1/4 cup flour in small bowl for topping. Cut in 5 tablespoons butter until crumbly. Sprinkle over filling. Bake at 350°F., 25 to 30 minutes or until golden and bubbly.

Mix together the cream and coffee. Microwave caramels until creamy and add to cream and coffee mixture. Stir in nuts and cinnamon. Pour into crust. Chill. Melt chocolate and drizzle on top.

This recipe is even better if you make your own graham cracker crust and use small tart pans to make individual caramel tarts. Enjoy!

Jennifer Templin **Cimarron-Memorial HS, Las Vegas, NV**

Chocolate & Peanut Butter Mousse Pie

Serves 6-8

7 whole graham crackers, crushed
1/4 cup unsalted butter, melted
2 tablespoons sugar
1 1/3 cups semisweet chocolate chips, (about 8 ounces)
2/3 cup whipping cream
2 tablespoons light corn syrup
1 teaspoon vanilla
6 ounces peanut butter chips, (about 1 cup)
3/4 cup whipping cream
2 tablespoons creamy peanut butter
1 teaspoon vanilla
1 cup whipping cream
2 tablespoons sugar

Preheat oven to 350 degrees. Spray a 9 inch glass pie dish with nonstick spray. Blend graham crackers, melted butter and sugar in food processor until moist clumps form. Press crumb mixture over bottom and up sides of prepared pie dish. Bake crust until lightly browned, about 15 minutes. Meanwhile, combine chocolate chips, cream, corn syrup and vanilla in microwave-safe bowl. Microwave on medium heat until chocolate softens, about 3 minutes. Whisk mixture until smooth. Spread chocolate mixture over bottom of baked crust. Freeze 10 minutes or until chocolate mixture is set. Microwave peanut butter chips and cream in large microwave-safe bowl on medium heat until chips soften, stirring often. Whisk in peanut butter and vanilla. Set aside to cool. In medium mixing bowl beat whipping cream using electric mixer until soft peaks form. Add sugar. Beat for 1 minute. Fold whipped cream mixture into peanut butter mixture. Spoon over chocolate layer. Chill at least 3 hours or up to a day. For added decoration, drizzle melted semisweet chocolate over top in crisscross directions.

Betty Wells **Bidwell JHS, Chico, CA**

Chocolate Layer Pie

Serves 15-20

3/4 cup butter, melted
1 1/2 cups flour, sifted
1 cup nuts, chopped
1 (8 ounce) package cream cheese, softened
1 (4-4 1/2 ounce) carton refrigerated dairy topping
1 cup confections' sugar
1 (3 3/4 ounce) instant vanilla pudding
1 (3 3/4 ounce) instant chocolate pudding
2 cups milk
1 (4-4 1/2 ounce) carton refrigerated dairy topping

Preheat oven to 350 degrees. Combine first 3 ingredients and press into bottom of 9 x 13 pan. Bake for 20 to 30 minutes. Cool. Combine next 3 ingredients and spread over cooled crust. Combine puddings and milk and spread over cream cheese layer. Top with refrigerated dairy topping. If desired, you can sprinkle chopped nuts or grated chocolate on top to garnish.

Celeste Giron — **Riverton HS, Riverton, UT**

Chocolate Mousse Pie

Serves 8-12

Filling:
1 package chocolate graham crackers
1/2 cup butter, melted
1 1/2 cups whipping cream
1 (12 ounce) package chocolate chips
5 egg yolks
2 teaspoons vanilla

Whipped Cream Topping:
1 cup whipping cream
1 teaspoon vanilla
4 tablespoons powdered sugar

Crush graham crackers in a large Ziploc bag that has been closed securely; use a meat hammer or a rolling pin. Mix crushed graham crackers with the melted butter. Press across the bottom and up the sides of a 9 inch spring form pan or a large pie pan, to form the pie crust. Chill for 1 hour. Heat whipping cream on medium heat on stove until small bubbles form, but do not let boil. Place chocolate chips, egg yolks, and vanilla into blender or food processor. Pour hot cream into blender and blend until smooth. Pour chocolate mixture into pie pan or spring form pan. Chill for at least 2 hours. Can be served with a dollop of whipped cream topping. Whip all ingredients for topping together until stiff peaks form.

This recipe is quick and easy, plus you can use different types of chips, if you don't like chocolate chips!

Carissa McCrory — **Whitney HS, Rocklin, CA**

Chocolate Pecan Pie

Serves 8-10

1 unbaked pie crust
10 ounces dark chocolate
3 large eggs
1 cup light brown sugar
1 cup evaporated milk
1 teaspoon vanilla
$1/4$ cup butter, melted
2 cups shelled pecans, chopped
whipped cream for topping

Preheat oven to 375 degrees. Prick bottom of pie crust and bake at 375 degrees for 8 minutes or until golden brown. Cool. Reduce heat to 325 degrees. Chop chocolate into small pieces. Place chocolate in double boiler and heat over boiling water. Set melted chocolate aside. In large mixing bowl, beat eggs until frothy. Add brown sugar and stir to mix. Slowly add evaporated milk, vanilla, and melted butter. Stir in melted chocolate, whisking to incorporate all ingredients. Pour into pie shell. Sprinkle with pecans. Bake for one hour. Serve with whipped cream.

This pie is fantastic. A real crowd pleaser, especially if you love rich chocolate desserts. Enjoy!

Patti Bartholomew — **Casa Roble HS, Orangevale, CA**

Cinnamon Apple Crostata

Serves 6

$1/2$ cup sugar
4 teaspoons cornstarch
2 teaspoons cinnamon
4 cups apples, peeled, thinly sliced (4 medium)
1 8-inch unbaked pie crust
1 teaspoon sugar

Preheat oven to 450 degrees. In medium bowl, combine $1/2$ cup sugar, cornstarch and cinnamon; blend well. Add apples; toss gently. Roll out pie crust and place on an ungreased cookie sheet. Spoon apple mixture onto center of crust, leaving a 2-inch border. Fold edge of crust 2 inches over apple mixture; crimp slightly. Brush crust edge with water; sprinkle with 1 teaspoon sugar. Bake for 15 minutes or until crust is golden brown. If necessary, cover crust with foil to prevent excessive browning. Bake an additional 5-15 minutes or until apples are tender. Cool 30 minutes before serving.

This easy recipe was given to me by my sister, Debbie. It's great for apple pie lovers who don't want all the calories from a 2-crust pie.

Diane Castro — **Temecula Valley HS, Temecula, CA**

Cinnamon Roll Ups

Makes 4 cups filling

1 loaf of sliced white sandwich bread
8 ounces cream cheese, softened
1 egg yolk
1 cup sugar, divided
2 teaspoons cinnamon
1 cube margarine, melted

Trim crust off bread. Roll bread flat with rolling pin. Mix cream cheese, egg yolk and 1/2 cup sugar. Spread on bread and roll each piece up tightly. Mix remaining sugar with cinnamon. Melt margarine and brush on each roll, then dip in cinnamon sugar mixture. Bake roll ups on a greased cookie sheet at 400 degrees for 9-12 minutes.

Everyone loves these! Taste a lot like a churro.

Valerie Veigel **Clearfield HS, Clearfield, UT**

Crunch Top Apple Pie

Serves 6-8

pastry dough for a double crust 9 inch pie, homemade, frozen, or refrigerated

Filling:
3/4 cup sugar
3 tablespoons flour
1 teaspoon cinnamon
dash salt
5 medium Granny Smith apples; peeled, cored and chopped
1 (16 ounce) jar cinnamon applesauce
1 tablespoon lemon juice
2 tablespoons butter, chopped into small pieces

Crunch Topping:
3 tablespoons flour
1/4 cup brown sugar
3 tablespoons butter, room temperature
vanilla ice cream, for serving

Preheat oven to 425 degrees. Line a 9 inch pie plate with half of the pastry dough. (I use Pillsbury refrigerated crusts; they are easy to unroll and taste great!) Combine sugar, flour, cinnamon and salt in a large bowl. Stir in the apples, applesauce, and lemon juice. Spoon mixture into pastry lined pie pan and dot with butter. Cut remaining crust into strips; arrange in a lattice design over the top of the pie. If strips extend beyond the edges of the bottom crust, tuck them under and gently pinch together, then flute edges of crust all the way around. For crunch topping, combine flour and sugar in a small bowl. Using a fork, cut in butter until mixture is crumbly. Sprinkle topping over top of lattice crust. Bake for 10 minutes, then reduce heat to 350 degrees and continue baking for 45-55 minutes, or until crust and topping are golden brown. Serve warm with vanilla ice cream.

Penny Niadna shared a similar version of this recipe with me at Thanksgiving, and I loved it so much that I made it for my family and friends five different times between Thanksgiving and New Year's this year!

Carole Delap — Golden West HS, Visalia, CA

Dried Fruit Pie

Serves 8

Crust: (makes 4 or 5 thin crusts)
4 cups flour
1 3/4 cups Crisco
1 teaspoon salt
1/2 cup ice water
1 egg, beaten
1 tablespoon vinegar
Filling:
1 cup each dried apricots, dried dates, dried plums (prunes)
1 1/2 cups water
1/2 teaspoon salt
1 (6 ounce) can frozen pineapple/orange juice or orange juice
1 teaspoon vanilla
1 prepared pastry shell, unbaked with
more pastry for the top (above recipe)
milk or egg whites and cinnamon for topping

Mix flour, Crisco, and salt together with a pastry blender. Mix ice water, egg, and vinegar together before adding to the dry ingredients. Use enough dough to line a 9-inch pie pan on bottom and sides. Use more dough to roll a 10-inch circle. Cut strips to use for lattice top. (Remaining dough can be shaped into balls and frozen until needed). Chop dried fruit. Combine all fruit, water, and salt; cook until all water is absorbed. Add frozen juice concentrate (not diluted) and vanilla. Pour filling into pastry shell and top with lattice strips. Tuck edges under on rim and crimp slightly. Brush with milk or egg white and cinnamon. Bake at 400 degrees for about 40-45 minutes, or until lattice strips are golden brown. May be served slightly warm or cool and serve with whipped cream.

This recipe came from my grandmother's neighbor. She was a lovely lady and a great cook. This pie is intensely fruity and wonderful.

Rebecca Bolt — Bear Creek HS, Stockton, CA

Dutch Apple Pie

Serves 6-8

1 (9 inch, deep dish) pie crust, unbaked
Filling:
6 cups Granny Smith apples, thinly sliced (about 5 medium)
3/4 cup sugar
1/2 cup brown sugar, packed
3 tablespoons flour
dash nutmeg
1 teaspoon cinnamon
dash salt
Crumb Topping:
1 cup flour
1/2 cup brown sugar, packed
1/2 cup unsalted butter,cold and firm,
cut into small pieces (not margarine)

Filling: Peel, core and slice apples, or use an apple peeler, corer, slicer. Stir together sugars, flour, nutmeg, cinnamon and salt in a large mixing bowl. Add apples and mix thoroughly coating all the slices. Turn apples into pie crust, including all the extra juices left in the bottom of the bowl. For *Topping:* Mix the flour, sugar and cold butter pieces together with a pastry blender or two knives until crumbly. (Cutting the butter into pieces before mixing with the flour and sugar will make it easier to cut in). Place topping evenly over apples, covering completely. Bake the pie at 425 degrees for 12 minutes only. Reduce oven temperature to 350 degrees and bake 40 minutes or until apples are tender and juices are bubbling at the edge of pie. Cover pie with foil if any portion begins to brown excessively. Cool on wire rack. Serve with vanilla ice cream.

This is an easy, delicious pie. My students make their own crust, but a Marie Calender's prepared crust works well, too.
I've tweaked this recipe over the years and finally gotten it just right!

Beckie Bloemker **Foothill HS, Sacramento, CA**

Ice Cream Pineapple Pie

Serves 6-8

1 baked and cooled 9" pie crust or 1 9" graham cracker pie crust
Filling:
1 cup milk
1 (4 serving) package vanilla instant pudding
1 pint (2 cups) vanilla ice cream, softened
Glaze:
1 (20 ounce) can crushed pineapple, packed in juice, divided
1 tablespoon sugar
1 tablespoon cornstarch or 2 teaspoons arrowroot

Filling: Combine milk, vanilla instant pudding and ice cream in a large bowl. Beat slowly 2 minutes or until well blended. Pour into prepared crust; refrigerate while you make the glaze. *Glaze:* Drain the pineapple, saving the juice. In a saucepan, mix 1/4 cup pineapple juice, sugar and cornstarch or arrowroot until smooth. Stir in another 1/4 cup juice and the drained crushed pineapple. Bring to a boil over medium heat, stirring constantly, until thick and clear. If it seems too thick, add a little more juice. Refrigerate until cold. Spread evenly over chilled pie. Chill about 1 hour before serving.

This recipe was given to me by my friend, Carol Norberg, years ago. We met at CSU San Jose. It is especially nice in the summer but good anytime.

Maureen Tolson **Lompoc Valley MS, Lompoc, CA**

Macaroon Pie

Serves 6-8

12 graham crackers or soda crackers
12 dates, finely chopped
1/2 cup pecans, chopped
1 cup sugar
1/4 teaspoon baking powder
3 egg whites, stiffly beaten
1 teaspoon almond extract

Preheat oven to 350 degrees. Mix together crackers, dates, pecans, sugar and baking powder. Fold into stiffly beaten egg whites and almond extract. Pour into well buttered pie plate; bake for 30 minutes.

My grandmother's recipe; easy to make and always a hit!

Beth Leighton **Helix Charter HS, La Mesa, CA**

Marvelous Cheese Pie

Serves 6-8

Crust:
1/3 cup margarine, melted
1 1/2 cups graham cracker crumbs
Filling:
12 ounces cream cheese, softened
1/2 cup sugar
1 teaspoon vanilla
Topping:
2 tablespoons cornstarch
2 tablespoons sugar
1 can fruit (raspberry, blueberry, boysenberry, cherries, etc.)

Preheat oven to 300 degrees. *Pie Crust:* Mix together the melted margarine and crumbs and press into a 9 inch pie pan. Set aside. *Filling:* Cream together the cream cheese, sugar, and vanilla until light and fluffy, about 8 minutes on medium with an electric mixer. Spread the filling across the crumb pie crust. Bake for 40 minutes or until the top looks somewhat dry. Remove from the oven and cool. *Topping:* While the filling is baking, use a saucepan and combine the cornstarch and sugar with a spoon. Add the fruit, including the liquid. Cook over medium heat, stirring constantly, until the mixture thickens. It should drop from the spoon in clumps. When the filling is cool, spread the cooled filling across the top of the pie. Refrigerate for at least four hours. The baked filling can be frozen to use in the future. *Add the fruit topping* once the filling has defrosted.

I have often tripled this recipe and made it in a large rectangular pan.
It will serve at least 30 people.

Jeanette Gehrke — **Serrano HS, Phelan, CA**

Plum Tart

Serves 6-8

2 cups all purpose flour
3/4 cup walnuts, finely chopped
3/4 cup light brown sugar, lightly packed
1 1/2 sticks butter, cold, cubed
1 egg yolk
2 pounds firm plums, pitted and quartered
whipping cream or Cool Whip, for topping

Preheat oven to 400 degrees. Combine the flour, walnuts, and sugar in a large mixing bowl. Add the butter and egg yolk. Mix with an electric mixer until crumbly. Press 1 1/2 cups of the crumb mixture in an even layer into the bottom of a 9 inch spring form or tart pan. Arrange plums in the pan, skin side down, to form a flower pattern; begin at the outside and work your way in. Sprinkle the rest of the crumb mixture evenly over the plums. Bake the tart for 40-50 minutes, or until lightly browned. Remove from oven and cool for 10 minutes. Remove pan and transfer to a flat plate. Serve warm or at room temperature. Top with whipping cream or Cool Whip.

I also use Granny Smith apples instead of plums.

Linda Brayton — **Grace Davis HS, Modesto, CA**

Simple Scones

Makes 8

2 cups flour
1/3 cup sugar
1 teaspoon baking powder
1/4 teaspoon baking soda
1/2 teaspoon salt
8 tablespoons unsalted butter, *frozen*
1/2 cup dried cranberries, raisins or currants
1/2 cup sour cream
1 large egg

Adjust oven rack to lower-middle position and preheat oven to 400 degrees. In a medium bowl, mix flour, sugar, baking powder, baking soda, and salt. Grate butter into flour mixture on the large holes of a box grater; use your finger to work in butter; mixture should resemble coarse meal, then stir in cranberries. In a small bowl, whisk sour cream and egg until smooth. Using a fork, stir sour cream mixture into flour mixture until large dough clumps form. Use your hands to press the dough against the bowl into a ball. (The dough will be sticky in places and there may not seem to be enough liquid at first, but as you press, the dough will come together.) Place on a lightly floured surface and pat into a 7-8 inch circle about 3/4 inch thick. Sprinkle with remaining teaspoon of sugar. Use a sharp knife to cut into 8 triangles; place on a cookie sheet (preferably lined with parchment paper), about 1 inch apart. Bake until golden, about 15-17 minutes. Cool for 5 minutes and serve warm or at room temperature.

These were an excellent product for students to make. My students loved them! Many made Cranberry-Orange and Lemon-Blueberry scones by using cranberries and blueberries with a teaspoon of zest. I even had chocolate chip scones! This dough compliments many flavors.

Lorie Bagley **Mt. Whitney HS, Visalia, CA**

Snohomish Pumpkin Pie

Makes 2 pies

First Step Ingredients:
1 1/2 cups sugar
2 teaspoons cinnamon
1/2 cup brown sugar
1 teaspoon ginger
1 teaspoon salt
1/2 teaspoon cloves
Second Step Ingredients:
2 (15 ounce) cans pumpkin
1 1/2 cups evaporated milk
4 eggs
1 cup milk
2 unbaked 9-inch pie crusts

Mix all *first step* ingredients together in a large bowl, making sure any and all clumps are out. (You don't want to bite into a clump of ginger! Trust me!) It is best to use your hands to mix it, and de-clump it all. *Second step ingredients;* Mix together in separate bowl. Slowly mix liquid ingredients with dry ingredients, using a mixer. Slow is the key because it will splash. For best results, let this sit for awhile before baking. It helps the flavors and seasonings to blend with the pumpkin. Pour into two 9 inch pie shells. Bake at 375 degrees for 30 minutes. Reduce heat to 350 degrees and bake for another 30 minutes, or until a knife comes clean when touched in the center.

Allowing the spices to mingle with the pumpkin makes this the most flavorful pie I have ever eaten.

Gay Quinn **Jordan HS, Sandy, UT**

Sweet Potato Pie

Serves 6-8

3 eggs, beaten
2/3 cup sugar
1/4 cup butter, melted
1/4 teaspoon nutmeg
1/4 teaspoon salt
1/4 teaspoon vanilla
1/2 teaspoon cinnamon
1 1/2 cups sweet potatoes, mashed
1/3 cup canned milk
1 (9 inch) pie crust, unbaked

Preheat oven to 425 degrees. Beat eggs and sugar together. Add melted butter, nutmeg, salt, vanilla, and cinnamon. Blend mashed sweet potatoes and canned milk. Mix well. Pour into unbaked pie shell and bake for 40 minutes. Then, bake at 350 degrees for 40 minutes. Serve plain or with whipped cream.

Yummy!

Alice Claiborne **Fairfield HS, Fairfield, CA**

Sweet Pumpkin-Apple Pie

Serves 6-8

Pecan Crunch Topping:
1/4 cup sugar
1/4 cup brown sugar
1/4 cup flour
1 teaspoon ground cinnamon
1/8 teaspoon salt
2/3 cup pecans, chopped
7 tablespoons unsalted butter, cut into pieces
Pumpkin Filling:
1/3 cup sugar
1/2 cup brown sugar
4 tablespoons flour
1 teaspoon ground cinnamon
2 teaspoons pumpkin pie spice
1/2 teaspoon salt
15 ounces solid pack pumpkin
2 eggs
8 ounces sour cream
Apple Layer:
2 tablespoons brown sugar
1/8 teaspoon ground cinnamon
1 teaspoon flour
2 medium Granny Smiths apples, peeled, cored and sliced 1/8 inch thick
1 tablespoon butter
2 tablespoons sugar

Place a baking sheet on the bottom shelf of the oven. Place the oven rack for the pie on the second level up from the bottom. Preheat the oven to 425 degrees. To make the pecan crunch topping; in a small bowl combine the sugars, flour, cinnamon, salt and pecans. Add the butter and using two knives or a pastry blender, cut in the butter until the mixture is crumbly. set aside. To make the pumpkin filling; in a small bowl stir together the sugars, flour, spices and salt. In a large bowl, mix the pumpkin, eggs and sour cream until smooth. Stir in the dry ingredients. To make the apple layer; in a large bowl, mix the brown sugar, cinnamon, and flour; toss with apples to coat evenly. In a 10 inch iron skillet, over medium heat, melt the butter. Sprinkle the sugar over the butter and cook 3 to 4 minutes, until just starting to brown; top with the apples and remove from heat. Pour the pumpkin filling over the apples and scatter the crunch topping over the top, leaving about a 1/4 inch border of pumpkin around the edges uncovered. Bake 10 minutes, then lower the oven temperature to 350 degrees. Bake about 40-45 minutes, until a knife inserted near the center comes out clean. Remove to a wire rack and cool at least 30 minutes. Serve warm with vanilla ice cream.

My dear friend, Cindy Bluethman, shared this recipe with me. This recipe is awesome.

Cari Sheridan — Grace Yokley MS, Ontario, CA

To Die for Peanut Butter Pie

Serves 8

1 pie crust, homemade, frozen, or refrigerated
1 cup whipping cream, whipped
1 pound cream cheese
1 cup sugar
3/4 cup peanut butter
1 jar milk chocolate topping
1 cup chocolate chips, melted
1/2 cup peanuts, finely chopped

Prepare pie crust according to pastry recipe or use a purchased crust. Whip the whipping cream till whip cream texture. Cream together cream cheese, sugar, and peanut butter thoroughly. Fold this mixture into the whipped cream. Coat bottom of pie crust with chocolate from jar. Top with filling. Melt chocolate chips and drizzle over pie. Sprinkle with peanuts. Let pie settle in the refrigerator for 3 to 4 hours or put in the freezer for 1 hour. Serve small pieces; pie is rich.

This simple pie is delicious and loved by all!

Linda Morris — Sultana HS, Hesperia, CA

Puddings & Custards

Apple Bread Pudding

Serves 8-12

1 pound golden delicious apples (or other eating apples)
2 tablespoons butter
1 1/4 cups sugar, divided
1/4 cup raisins
1/4 cup apple cider
12-14 slices French baguette, sliced approximately 1/4 inch thick
3 egg yolks
2 eggs
1 teaspoon vanilla
1 cup half and half
3 cups 2% milk
powdered sugar for sprinkling over the top

Preheat oven to 400 degrees. Peel the apples and core the apples; cut into quarters; slice very thin. Heat the butter in a large skillet and add the apple slices. Sprinkle with 1/4 cup sugar; sauté for 2 minutes over medium heat. Add the raisins and the apple cider. Cook until bubbly; remove from heat. Arrange the bread slices, slightly overlapping, over the bottom of a 9 x 12 inch glass baking dish. Do not crowd the bread; use only enough to cover the bottom of the pan in one layer. Spoon the apple mixture evenly over the bread. Blend the egg yolks and the eggs with the remaining cup of sugar, vanilla, half & half, and milk. Beat lightly and pour over the apples and bread slices. Bake for 40 minutes. Remove from oven and cool slightly. Sprinkle powdered sugar over the top while still lukewarm. Serve warm.

Mary Makela — **Fort Bragg HS, Fort Bragg, CA**

Blender Chocolate Mousse

Serves 4-6

6 ounces semi-sweet chocolate chips
3 tablespoons hot coffee
1-2 tablespoons rum or brandy,
can substitute 1- 2 teaspoons rum or brandy flavoring
1/2 cup whole milk, scalded
2 eggs

Put all ingredients in a blender and blend on high speed for 2 minutes. Pour into serving dishes and chill. Make early in the day or night before so flavors can develop. Serve with a dollop of whipped cream. Can garnish with chocolate shavings.

This mousse has a lighter and more airy texture than the typical recipe; a delicious & quick dessert.

Jackie Williams — **Prospect HS, Saratoga, CA**

Chocolate Dream

Serves 12-16

Crust:
1/2 cup butter
1 cup flour
1 cup walnuts, chopped
Filling:
1 pint heavy whipping cream
1/2 cup sugar
1 teaspoon vanilla
1 cup powdered sugar
8 ounces cream cheese
Pudding:
2 cups sugar
6 tablespoons flour
2 tablespoons cocoa
3 cups warm milk
12 ounces evaporated milk
2 egg yolks, beaten
2 tablespoons butter
1 teaspoon vanilla
1/2 cup walnuts, chopped

Crust: Preheat the oven to 350 degrees. Using a food processor or pastry blender, gently mix butter, flour, and walnuts. Press into a 9 x 13 cake pan; a glass pan makes for a nicer presentation. Bake for 20 minutes or until golden brown. Cool and chill. *Cream Filling:* Place heavy whipping cream in a mixing bowl with high sides. Add sugar and vanilla. Whip on high until stiff (do not over beat, or you will create sweet butter). Mix 1 cup of the whipped cream with powdered sugar and cream cheese. Spread over cooled crust. Set aside remaining whipped cream. *Pudding:* Pour sugar in a large saucepan; stir in flour and cocoa. Slowly add warm milk to pan, a little at a time. Add evaporated milk and egg yolks. Heat over medium heat, stirring constantly until thickened. Remove from heat and add butter and vanilla. Cool and chill. Spread over cream filling. *Topping:* Spread remaining whipped cream over pudding. Sprinkle with chopped walnuts. Chill.

This was a Christmas tradition at my mom's house while I was growing up.
Yes, you could use instant pudding and cool whip
but you would miss out on the creamy richness.

DeLisa Davis — **Sutter Union HS, Sutter, CA**

Chocolate Mousse

Serves 4-6

2 cups heavy cream, divided
1 cup semisweet chocolate, finely chopped
1/4 cup powdered sugar, sifted
1 teaspoon vanilla extract
dark chocolate and white chocolate curls for decoration

In a small saucepan, heat 1/2 cup cream to almost boiling. Remove from heat and stir in chocolate. Cover with a lid and let sit for 5 minutes. Remove lid and stir until smooth. Place mixture in a large metal bowl. In another large bowl with an electric mixer, beat 1 1/2 cups cream until thickened. Add powdered sugar and vanilla extract. Continue beating until stiff peaks form. Gently fold 1/3 of whipped cream into chocolate mixture. When combined, fold in the remaining whipped cream. Pour into cups. Chill in refrigerator for best consistency. Decorate with chocolate curls before serving.

So quick and easy to prepare. The students love this recipe.
Very elegant when served in stemmed glasses!

Doreen Lee — **Frances Ellen Watkins Harper JHS, Davis, CA**

Leche Flan

Serves 6-8

1/4-1/3 cup sugar, granulated
1 dozen egg yolks
3/4 cups sugar
1 teaspoon vanilla
1 can evaporated milk (not condensed!)
1/2 teaspoon lemon zest
9 inch cake pan, round or heart-shaped are most attractive
9 x 13, or larger baking pan in which the 9" pan can easily nest

Preheat oven to 350 degrees. The beginning step of this recipe is the only challenge. Using tongs to hold the pan, caramelize the bottom of the cake pan (must be heavy duty) with 1/4-1/3 cup sugar by heating it over low to medium heat until sugar melts completely. Remove pan from heat the instant sugar begins to bubble or brown (or sugar will burn immediately, and you'll have to begin again)! Set aside to cool while preparing the flan. Sugar will crackle as it cools; it's fun to hear and watch! Into large mixing bowl, pour separated egg yolks (save egg whites for angel food cake or meringue?). Add remaining 3/4 cup sugar and vanilla, beating until smooth. Add evaporated milk and lemon zest, beating until bubbly/fluffy. Pour flan mixture into caramelized pan. Sugar will crack like crazy! Place this round flan pan **carefully** into larger baking pan that is filled halfway with water (think: large baking pan as a bathtub with round flan pan "floating" inside). Place both pans (flan nested inside larger pan) carefully into center of oven. Bake at least 50 minutes (usually 60-70 minutes) at 350 degrees. Test center of flan for doneness (inserted table knife must be absolutely clean). Remove flan from larger bath pan to cool. Refrigerate (covered with plastic wrap) until serving. Tastes richer if flan is prepared a day or two ahead of serving. *To serve:* Gently slice any flan edges that adhere to side of pan (flan should wiggle free of pan). Place serving platter (with a rim that is 2" larger than flan pan) on top of flan pan. Working over sink, **quickly** flip pan upside down. This allows caramelized sugar (a pretty golden brown) to be visible.

Leche Flan, a traditional custard dessert, was introduced by the conquering Spanish. This particular (treasured family) recipe makes a dense (heavier) flan than is commonly served elsewhere. Also note, that "flan" is typically pronounced "Plan" by most Filipinos ("Pilipinos").

Beth Pool — Ann Sobrato HS, Morgan Hill, CA

Old Fashioned Bread Pudding

Serves 12-16

1/2 cup butter
6 cups milk
8 eggs, beaten
2 tablespoons vanilla extract
2 cups granulated sugar
1 teaspoon salt
1 1/2 tablespoons cinnamon
1 loaf sliced white bread, cut into cubes
1 cup raisins
1/2 cup walnuts, chopped
2 small Granny Smith apples, chopped
1 cup maple syrup

Preheat oven to 350 degrees. Generously grease a 9 x 13 cake pan. Using a large sauce pan, combine butter and milk; heat just below a boil. In a large mixing bowl beat eggs thoroughly. Combine vanilla, sugar, salt, cinnamon and eggs; mix well. Pour warm milk into egg mixture and stir. Cut bread slices into quarters and stack into greased pan. Sprinkle bread with raisins, chopped walnuts and apple. Pour hot liquid over bread pieces. Cover with aluminum foil and bake for 45-55 minutes or until a knife comes out clean. Remove foil after 30 minutes of baking. Let cool about 20 minutes and pour maple syrup over the top of the pudding and serve warm.

This dessert is always a hit around the holidays. A great substitution is to replace the raisins with dried cranberries and pecans for the walnuts.

Very tasty when served with fresh whipped cream or vanilla ice cream.

Tanya Wright — Pitman HS, Turlock, CA

Recipe Index

Cookies

Frozen Desserts

Fruits, Cobblers & Gelatin

Pies & Pastries

For additional copies of *this* book,
and our *other* cookbook titles,
please visit our website:

www.creativecookbook.com

Or, use the re-order forms below.

CREATIVE Cookbook

Great Beginnings
Sweet Endings

Please send me _____ copy(ies) of *Great Beginnings•Sweet Endings* at **$12.00** ea. (includes tax and shipping). Make checks payable to Creative Cookbook Company. Mail this form with your check to: **8332 Brush Drive, Huntington Beach, CA 92647**

Enclosed is my check for _____ book(s) at **$12.00** ea $________.

Name ______________________________

Address ______________________________

City ________________ State ______ Zip __________

CREATIVE Cookbook

Great Beginnings
Sweet Endings

Please send me _____ copy(ies) of *Great Beginnings•Sweet Endings* at **$12.00** ea. (includes tax and shipping). Make checks payable to Creative Cookbook Company. Mail this form with your check to: **8332 Brush Drive, Huntington Beach, CA 92647**

Enclosed is my check for _____ book(s) at **$12.00** ea $________.

Name ______________________________

Address ______________________________

City ________________ State ______ Zip __________

Great Beginnings

appetizers • dips • salsas • snacks

Compiled by
FACS (Home Economics) Teachers

Editor
Gerry Murry Henderson

Graphic Design, Typography & Production
Mike Burk Production Services, Long Beach, CA

Visit us at: www.creativecookbook.com

ISBN 0-914159-23-2

1/110M062007/MBPS/DPS

Thank you for purchasing this book. The sale helps raise much needed money for school programs. And, a big thanks to the Family & Consumer Science and Home Economics Teachers for donating all the quality recipes.

TEACHER ADVISORY COMMITTEE

Kathie Baczynski
Mt. Carmel HS, San Diego, CA

Priscilla Burns
Pleasant Valley HS, Chico, CA

Neva Clauson
Lebanon HS, Lebanon, OR

Diane Cluff
Provo HS, Provo, UT

Jamie Davis
Redwood IS, Thousand Oak, CA

Carole Delap
Golden West HS, Visalia, CA

Peg Ellington
Yucca Valley HS, Yucca Valley, CA

Pam Ford
Temecula Valley HS, Temecula, CA

Maria Fregulia
Lassen HS, Susanville, CA

La Rae Hargues
Hesperia HS, Hesperia, CA

Debbie Harvey
Amador Valley HS, Pleasanton, CA

Gerry Murry Henderson
Temple City HS, Temple City, CA

Camille Hicks
Riverton HS, Riverton, UT

Reiko Ikkanda
So. Pasadena MS, So. Pasadena, CA

Mary Lash
Paramount HS, Paramount, CA

Jan Martin
Reed HS, Sparks, NV

Leilani Neiner
Mesquite HS, Gilbert, AZ

Ann Porter
San Luis Obispo HS, SLO, CA

Betty Rabin-Fung
Sierra Vista JHS, Canyon Country, CA

April Rosendahl
Chino HS, Chino, CA

Sonja Shumaker
Ayala HS, Chino Hills, CA

Karen Tilson
Poly HS, Riverside, CA

Betty Wells
Bidwell JHS, Chico, CA

Kathryn P. Whitten
Home Economics Education, Fresno, CA

Thanks to the following people for working hard to provide a good product and a simple, successful fundraiser. We couldn't do it without you!

Gerry Henderson, our editor, teaches full time and goes over every recipe to ensure there aren't any errors. **Sue Russell** and **Betty Rabin-Fung** spend many hours typing and proofing. Providing great customer service are **Roger Upperman, Ron Rouintree, Danny Hawes,** and **Jason Medina. Tim Campbell, Marc Trimble,** and **Grady Reed** travel throughout the Western U.S., helping teachers to be successful with their sales. **Mike Burk** designs the book, does the layout and makes it "printable". We're proud to print our books with **Jerry Bernstein** and **Delta Printing Solutions** in Valencia, California. And, a special thanks to **Shelley Herrema** for the "flip-over" book idea!

Sincerely,

Doug Pierce and ***Doug Herrema,*** owners, **Creative Cookbook Company**

To reorder this and other books, visit our website at www.creativecookbook.com, or use the re-order form on page 160.

Great Beginnings

Table of Contents

Flip This Book Over for
Sweet Endings

Table of Contents

Cover Photo for *Great Beginnings:*

Polenta Crostini with Ham & Wisconsin Asiago

Makes 12

9 thin slices cured ham
2 11-ounce tubes refrigerated polenta with sun-dried tomato
3/4 cup (3 ounces) Wisconsin Asiago cheese, shredded
1 large Roma tomato, seeded and chopped
2 Tablespoons pine nuts, toasted and coarsely chopped
2 Tablespoons snipped fresh basil or 1/2 tsp. dried basil
2 Tablespoons Sundried tomato-flavored mayonnaise
Nonstick cooking spray as needed

Coat a baking sheet with nonstick cooking spray. Slice each tube of polenta into 6 slices. Arrange slices on baking sheet. With a small spoon, scoop out shallow depression in each slice. Spray slices light with nonstick cooking spray. Bake for 20 minutes. In a small bowl, combine Asiago cheese, Roma tomato, pine nuts, and basil. Set aside. Stack three slices of ham and cut into quarters, keeping stacks intact. Repeat twice. To assemble, spoon some of the cheese mixture into depressions in polenta slices. Top each polenta slice with about 1/2 teaspoon of the tomato-flavored mayonnaise. Add a stack of ham slice quarters to each polenta slice. Top each with some of the remaining cheese mixture. Return the crostini to oven and heat 2-3 minutes or until cheese is slightly melted.

Recipe and photo courtesy of National Pork Board

Cold Appetizers

Antipasto Stuffed Baguette

Makes about 25

2 (14-inch) baguettes
1 bunch fresh basil, rinsed and stems removed
9 ounces sliced dry salami
4 ounces goat cheese, chilled
1 cup black olives
14 ounces artichoke hearts
10 ounces roasted red peppers

Cut "V" shaped slice out of the entire length of each baguette. Remove small amount of bread inside and set aside. Place basil leaves along inside of baguette. Layer the salami slices on top of the basil. Crumble the goat cheese on top of the salami. Mince the olives finely, almost to a paste, and spread them across the goat cheese. Thinly slice the artichoke hearts, placing them along the length of the baguettes. Chop the roasted red peppers and layer them last. Cover this with the reserved "V" shaped slice. Wrap tightly and place in the refrigerator for an hour to firm. Remove from wrap and slice evenly into 1 or 2-inch pieces.

This is a recipe I received years ago from a senior student. It's delicious, easy, unique and loved by kids and adults.

Margo Olsen — **Amador Valley HS, Pleasanton, CA**

BBQ Chinese Pork

Serves 6-8

2 pound pork tenderloin
6 cloves fresh garlic, finely minced
2 tablespoons fresh ginger, minced
2 teaspoons salt
2 tablespoons soy sauce
$1/4$ cup honey
1 cup sherry
1 cup vegetable stock
1 tablespoon 5-spice powder

Place all marinade ingredients (not the pork) in a saucepan and bring just to a simmer. Simmer 2-3 minutes to dissolve the honey. Cool until cold. Place the

pork and marinade in a plastic bag together and marinade 24 hours. Prepare a grill. Cook over indirect grill or fire until well done. Cool completely. Slice very thinly to serve.

Excellent cold with plum, hoisin, mustard sauces and sesame seeds. For a traditional red BBQ add a couple drops of red dye or several red raspberries.

Priscilla Burns **Pleasant Valley HS, Chico, CA**

Bean Spread

Serves 4-6

1 can Cannelli beans, rinsed
1/2 can black olives
1 clove garlic, finely grated
1/4 cup lemon olive oil (or olive oil + 1 tablespoon lemon zest)
1/4 cup balsamic vinegar
1-2 teaspoons honey
salt & pepper, to taste
Crostini or wheat crackers

Blend all ingredients in a food processor. Serve on Crostini or wheat crackers

This recipe was created by Victoria Thibeau, our multi-talented Assistant Principal here at CVHS! It's inexpensive, quick, nutritious and delicious!

Peggy Herndon **Central Valley HS, Shasta Lake, CA**

Beef Blossoms

Serves 12-18

4 ounces cream cheese, softened
3-4 green onions, finely chopped
1-2 packages cooked beef, thinly sliced

Mix cream cheese and onions together. Place a dollop of mixture in middle of beef square. Gather beef square up by each corner and pinch together. Each appetizer resembles a flower in bloom. Chill until ready to serve.

This is an old family favorite!

Shelly J. Wellins **Bolsa Grande HS, Garden Grove, CA**

Beef Cheeseball

Serves 10-12

2 (8 ounce) packages cream cheese
2 tablespoons horseradish
1/2 cup green onions, diced
2 packages deli beef slices, diced
1 cup nuts, chopped (optional)

Soften cream cheese; stir in horseradish and green onions. Mix in diced beef. Shape into a ball and roll in nuts. Let sit for 2 hours. Serve with crackers.

Sherrie Hinton **Gilbert HS, Gilbert, AZ**

Blue Cheese Ball

Makes 2 1/2 cup ball

1 (8 ounce) package cream cheese
1 (4 ounce) package blue cheese, crumbled
1/4 cup butter or margarine
2/3 cup chopped olives
1 tablespoon chives or green onion tops, chopped
3/4 cup nuts, chopped

Combine all ingredients except nuts. Form into a softball-size ball. Roll ball in chopped nuts until completely covered. Chill for 2-3 hours or overnight to let flavors blend. Serve with assorted snack crackers.

A long time favorite at family and faculty parties.

Anne Hawes **Cottonwood HS, Murray, UT**

Caponata (Eggplant Appetizer)

Makes 8 cups

2 eggplants, peeled and cut into 1/2 inch cubes (8 cups)
salt
1/2 cup olive oil, divided
2 cups celery, finely chopped
3/4 cup onion, finely chopped
1/3 cup red wine vinegar
4 teaspoon sugar
3 cups Italian plum tomatoes, drained
2 tablespoons tomato paste
6 large green or black olives, pitted and sliced
2 tablespoons capers
2 teaspoons salt
1/4 cup toasted pine nuts
freshly ground black pepper
2 French baguettes
butter or margarine
Parmesan cheese, grated

Sprinkle the cubes of eggplant generously with salt and set them in a colander or large sieve over paper towels to drain. After about 30 minutes, pat the cubes dry with fresh paper towels and set them aside. In a heavy 12-14" skillet, heat 1/4 cup of the olive oil. Add the celery and cook over moderate heat, stirring frequently, for 10 minutes. Then stir in the onions and cook for another 8-10 minutes or until the celery and onions are soft and lightly colored. With a slotted spoon, transfer them to a bowl. Pour the remaining 1/4 cup olive oil into the skillet and, over high heat, sauté the eggplant cubes, stirring and turning them constantly for about 8 minutes or until they are lightly browned. Return the celery and onions to the skillet and stir in the vinegar, sugar, tomatoes, tomato paste, olives, capers and 2 teaspoons salt and a few grindings of pepper (to taste). Bring to a boil; reduce the heat and simmer uncovered, stirring frequently, for about 15 minutes. Remove from heat and stir in the pine nuts. Slice the baguettes into 1/2" slices; butter and sprinkle with the parmesan cheese.

Broil until nicely browned on each side. Serve the caponata at room temperature on the toasted baguettes.

This reads like a lot of work, but it goes very quickly and makes a wonderful appetizer. Larger servings can be used as a vegetarian main dish as well.

Pamela Bonilla — **Valley View HS, Moreno Valley, CA**

Cheese Spread

Makes 1 1/4 cups

1 cup sharp cheddar cheese, shredded
1 egg, hard cooked, chopped
1/4 cup dill pickle, minced
2 tablespoons green pepper, minced
1 tablespoon onion, minced
1 tablespoon pimiento, chopped
2 tablespoons mayonnaise

In a small mixing bowl combine cheese, egg, dill pickle, green pepper, onion, and pimiento; stir in mayonnaise. Cover and refrigerate over night. Serve with assorted crackers.

Leftovers make a great sandwich spread.

Cheri Schuette — **Valley View MS, Simi Valley, CA**

Crab & Shrimp Party Log

Makes 1 Log

1 (8 ounce) package cream cheese
1 can crab meat, drained and picked over
1 can shrimp, drained
2-3 tablespoons sherry
3 or more tablespoons fresh parsley, snipped

Mix all ingredients, except the parsley, together to form a log. Roll in parsley. Cover with saran wrap. Chill at least 2 hours, best if overnight. Serve with crackers

Another Mom recipe. They are always good!

Penny Childers — **Ramona HS, Ramona, CA**

Crab Stuffed Snow Peas

Makes 60

8 ounce package cream cheese, softened
1 tablespoon lemon juice
6 ounces snow crab meat, drained
Kosher salt and pepper, to taste
60 snow peas, ends trimmed
1 red pepper, cut into matchstick slivers

In a small bowl, mix softened cream cheese and lemon juice until smooth. Stir in crab; season with Kosher salt and pepper. Cook snow peas in boiling water for about 1 minute until wilted, but still crisp. Drain snow peas and drop into a bowl of cold water. Drain. With a sharp paring knife, split open the curved seam of

each snow pea (this may be done ahead of time). With a small spoon, fill each snow pea with crab mixture. Garnish with the sliver of red pepper.

Kathie Baczynski — **Mt. Carmel HS, Poway, CA**

Easy Cheese Ball

Makes 1 ball

2 (8 ounce) packages cream cheese, softened
1 Jar Kraft Roka Blue Cheese
2 Jars Kraft Old English Cheese
1 tablespoon dried onion
almond slices, optional

Mix all of the ingredients together using an electric mixer. Serve in a bowl with crackers or form into a ball and roll in sliced almonds.

This is a holiday favorite!

Karen Drummond — **Kearns HS, Kearns, UT**

Fresh Vegetable Pizza

Makes 2 medium pizzas

Nonstick pan spray
2 packages of Crescent Refrigerator Rolls
Sauce:
2 (8 ounce) packages cream cheese, softened
1 cup mayonnaise
1 package Hidden Valley Ranch Dressing mix
Topping:
1 cup cauliflower, finely chopped
1 cup yellow, red, &/or orange peppers, finely chopped
1 cup broccoli, finely chopped
1 cup green onions, finely chopped
1 cup cheddar cheese, grated
Options:
1 cup black olives,sliced
1 cup tomatoes, finely chopped and drained

Preheat oven to 425 degrees. Unroll crescent rolls and press dough flat onto a large sprayed pizza pan or 2 medium sprayed pizza pans. Bake for 10-15 minutes or follow the package directions. Baked pizza crust should be light golden brown. Cool. Sauce: Mix together cream cheese, mayonnaise, and Ranch dressing mix. Spread over baked and cooled pizza crust. Toppings: Combine in bowl cauliflower, peppers, broccoli, and green onions. Sprinkle vegetables over the dressing mixture like a pizza topping. Sprinkle with grated cheese and press all ingredients partly into the dressing mixture. Top with sliced olives and tomatoes, if desired. Chill until firm. Cut into pizza wedges or bite size pieces.

We like putting the cauliflower, peppers, broccoli and green onions through a salad shooter type machine to have a very fine mixed vegetable topping. Vegetables can be changed by likes and dislikes and availability. Dough and pizza crusts can be made ahead of time so multiple pizzas can be made to serve many.

Neva Clausen — **Lebanon HS, Lebanon, OR**

Garden Harvest Squares

Makes about 30-35

2 cans crescent rolls
1 (8 ounce) package low-fat cream cheese
1/2 cup low-fat sour cream
1 teaspoon dill weed
1/8 teaspoon garlic powder
2 cups total: broccoli florets, cauliflower florets, cucumber (seeded & diced), zucchini (seeded & diced), radish slices, and scallions (choose at least three of the above)

Preheat oven to 375 degrees. *Crust:* Line a 15 x 10 sheet pan with dough (unroll into long crescent rectangles). Press over the bottom and up the sides to form the crust; firmly press perforations to seal. Bake for 13 to17 minutes or until golden brown. Cool completely on wire rack. *Spread:* In a medium bowl, combine the cream cheese, sour cream, dill weed, and garlic powder; blend well. *Veggies:* Cut into small pieces. Spread cream mixture over entire crust, cover with veggies. Cut and serve.

I make & serve this one all of the time. Healthy and great tasting!

Leilani Neiner — **Mesquite HS, Gilbert, AZ**

Goat Cheese Appetizer

Serves 8

2-4 heads of garlic, roasted
1 loaf of crusty bread or crackers
1 (1 ounce) package goat cheese
2 tablespoons olive oil
2 tablespoons balsamic vinegar
2 teaspoons fresh thyme (optional)
2 teaspoons fresh basil (optional)
capers
sun dried tomatoes
sprigs of rosemary, chopped

Preheat oven to 400 degrees. To roast garlic; cut top of each head of garlic, peel off outside skin as much as possible, leaving head of garlic in tact. Put head of garlic on a piece of foil and sprinkle with olive oil, salt and pepper. Wrap foil around garlic and bake 1 hour until garlic is tender. On a large platter, arrange roasted garlic. Cut goat cheese into 1" pieces and arrange around garlic. In a small bowl, combine olive oil, balsamic vinegar, herbs, sun-dried tomatoes, salt and pepper. Drizzle over goat cheese and garlic. Garnish with capers and sprigs of rosemary. Serve with slices of bread or crackers.

This recipe was given to me by my friend Wanda Hicks. It is my most requested appetizer.

Michelle Miller — **Aliso Viejo HS, Aliso Viejo, CA**

Grandma's Fish Eyes

Serves 15-20

1 or 2 glass jars of Kraft Old English Cheese, depending on size of bread
1 loaf white bread, cut lengthwise
butter or margarine
small green olives with pimento, rinsed in cold water and dried

Open cheese and place in pan of hot water to soften. Cut off crust of bread. Place one slice of bread on piece of wax paper larger than the bread. Spread with margarine or butter. Spread with cheese and make a row of olives on the long edge of the bread, about 1/2 inch from the edge. Bring wax paper up and begin to roll, pressing as you roll. Twist the ends of wax paper. Place in freezer for a couple of hours or overnight. Leave out 1/2 to 3/4 of an hour to defrost. When ready (partially frozen), slice pieces about 1/2 inch thick. Place on serving tray; cover with saran wrap until ready to serve. *Note:* Do not use outside crusts of bread (first and last slices).

My grandma makes this every holiday. It is a family favorite. I hope you enjoy it as much as my family has over the years. Thanks, Grandma Sargent.

Christina Osbahr — **Delano HS, Delano, CA**

Hidden Valley Ranch Pinwheels

Makes 3 dozen

2 (8 ounces) packages cream cheese, softened
1 (1 ounce) package Hidden Valley Ranch Salad Dressing Mix
2 green onions, minced
4 (12 inch) flour tortillas
1 (4 ounce) jar pimientoes, diced
1 (4 ounce) can diced green chiles
1 (2.25 ounce) can black olives, sliced

Mix cheese, ranch mix, and green onions together and spread on tortillas. Drain vegetables and blot dry on paper towels. Sprinkle equal amounts of pimientoes, chiles, and olives on top of the cream cheese mixture. Roll tortillas tightly and cover or wrap in plastic wrap. Chill at least 2 hours. Cut rolls into 1 inch pieces, discarding ends. Serve with spirals facing up.

These are always a hit! Very tasty.

Monica Blanchette — **Landmark MS, Moreno Valley, CA**

Layered Goat Cheese Torta

Makes 3 cups

1 head garlic
olive oil
kosher salt and freshly cracked black pepper, to taste
1 (8 ounce) package cream cheese, room temperature
8 ounces goat cheese, room temperature
1/2 cup sun-dried tomato pesto
1/3 cup basil pesto

Slice top off head of garlic and drizzle with olive oil; sprinkle with salt and pepper. Wrap in foil and roast in a preheated 400 degree oven about 1 hour, until garlic is soft. Meanwhile, in bowl of a free-standing mixer fitted with a paddle attachment, cream together cheeses. Divide mixture evenly among 3 small bowls. Add sun-dried tomato pesto to one bowl and mix well. Add basil pesto to second bowl, mixing well. Squeeze roasted garlic cloves into third bowl. Season all 3 mixtures with salt and pepper. Line a 3 cup ramekin with dampened cheesecloth or plastic wrap,draping excess over rim. Spoon sun-dried tomato pesto mixture into bottom of mold and smooth with a rubber spatula. Top with roasted garlic mixture, and finish with basil pesto mixture, spreading evenly. Fold excess cheesecloth or plastic wrap over top. Refrigerate at least one hour or longer. To serve, unfold cheesecloth or plastic wrap, invert ramekin onto platter, remove and peel away cloth or plastic wrap. Serve with crackers or Melba toast.

A big hit at holiday parties. Can be made several days in advance.

Betty Rabin-Fung, Retired **Sierra Vista JHS, Canyon Country, CA**

Malia's Spicy Thai Chicken Wraps

Serves 10

1 pound boneless, skinless chicken breasts, cut into 1-inch pieces
1/3 cup chicken broth
2 tablespoons shallots, minced
2 tablespoons green onions, minced
1-2 tablespoons fish sauce
1 stalk fresh lemon grass, bottom 6 inches only, minced
2-4 red chiles, seeded and minced
2 tablespoons mint leaves, chopped
3 tablespoons fresh lime juice
salt to taste
10 butter lettuce leaves
Salsa (Nam Prik):
4 to 6 red chiles, seeded and chopped
6 cloves garlic, chopped
1 tablespoon brown sugar, or to taste
3 tablespoons fish sauce, or to taste
3 tablespoons fresh lime juice, or to taste
Garnish:
whole mint leaves
lime wedges
tomato wedges
cucumber slices

Prepare salsa by mixing all ingredients well. Refrigerate and allow flavor to blend. Heat a skillet over medium heat and add the chicken and broth and cook until chicken is no longer pink. Remove chicken and set aside to cool. Add shallots, green onions, and fish sauce to the pan. Stir for 1 minute. Remove from the heat. Mix together the chicken and the broth, shallot mixture, lemon grass, chiles, mint, and lime juice. If desired, season with salt. Arrange in the center of a lettuce leaf. Wrap the lettuce leaf around the chicken salad and eat with your

fingers, using the salsa as a dip. Garnish with whole mint leaves, lime wedges, tomato wedges and cucumber slices. If you wish to make this more of a main dish, add a little rice into your lettuce wrap.

One of my students demonstrated this dish and the audience raved about it.

Ann Porter **San Luis Obispo HS, San Luis Obispo, CA**

Marinated Cheese

Serves 16

1/2 cup olive oil
1/2 cup white wine vinegar
1 (2 ounce) jar diced pimentos, drained
3 tablespoons fresh parsley, chopped
3 tablespoons green onions, minced
3 cloves garlic, minced
1 teaspoon sugar
3/4 teaspoon dried whole basil
1/2 teaspoon salt
1/2 teaspoon fresh ground pepper
1 (8 ounce) brick sharp cheddar cheese (5 1/2 x 2 x 1)
1 (8 ounce) brick Monterey Jack cheese (5 1/2 x 2 x 1)
1(8 ounce) package cream cheese-chilled
fresh parsley for garnish

In a small bowl, whisk the olive oil, white wine vinegar, pimentos, parsley, green onions, garlic, sugar, basil, salt and pepper. Set aside. Slice the cheeses in 1/4 inch thick slices, put slices in a 9 x 13 inch pan. Pour marinade over the cheeses. Marinade 8 hours, turning approximately 4 times. Transfer to a serving dish, spoon over the marinade. Garnish with fresh parsley. Serve with assorted crackers.

A different way to serve sliced cheese, from my girlfriend Kristi, whom I have known since 2nd grade.

Chrisann Boone **Reedley HS, Reedley, CA**

Marinated Shrimp

Serves 12

2 pounds shrimp, cooked, shelled, deveined, and thawed (if needed)
1 medium red onion, thinly sliced
2 small lemons, sliced
1/2 cup black olives, pitted and sliced
1/2 cup olive or vegetable oil
3 tablespoons red wine vinegar
3 tablespoons lemon juice
1/3 cup parsley, chopped
1 clove garlic, halved
1 teaspoon dry mustard
1 teaspoon dried basil, crumbled
1 teaspoon salt
1/4 teaspoon black pepper

Layer shrimp, onions, lemon slices, and black olives in a medium size bowl. Combine oil, vinegar, lemon juice, parsley, garlic, dry mustard, basil, salt and pepper in a jar or container with tight fitting lid; cover and shake to blend well. Pour marinade over shrimp; toss gently. Cover and refrigerate over night, tossing occasionally. Serve chilled.

Wonderful appetizer; the first thing to go when I dish it out.

Shannon Kelly Smith — **Las Vegas HS, Las Vegas, NV**

Mediterranean Walnut Spread

Serves 10-20

1 (15 ounce) can garbanzo beans
1 cup walnuts, chopped
1 cup fresh basil, lightly packed
4 tablespoons olive oil
4-6 teaspoons lemon juice
1/4 teaspoon salt
1/4 teaspoon black pepper
2 slices lemon for garnish
sprig basil for garnish
toasted thin baguette slices or pita bread slices

Drain garbanzo beans, reserving liquid. In food processor bowl, combine beans and 4 tablespoons of reserved liquid. Add walnuts, basil, olive oil, lemon juice and salt and pepper. Cover and blend or process until nearly smooth. Scrape down sides and add additional liquid if mixture is stiff. Spoon into a serving dish and garnish the center with lemon slices and a sprig of basil. Serve with toasted baguette or pita slices. To store, place in an airtight container in refrigerator for up to 5 days.

A larger serving of this could be an interesting alternative to the ordinary sandwich. This spread contains healthy fats from the olive oil and walnuts. Recent studies have shown that a switch to the Mediterranean style of eating is beneficial to heart health.

Laurie Paolozzi — **West HS, Torrance, CA**

Olive Curry Spread

Serves 8

2 cups medium cheddar cheese, grated
1 (small) can chopped black olives
2 green onions, finely chopped
1 clove garlic, minced
1/2 cup mayonnaise
1/2 teaspoon curry

Mix above ingredients and refrigerate 4-12 hours to blend flavors. Serve on sliced baguette or wheat thins.

This recipe is from my friend, Meredith Castro, who is a great cook!

Pat Hufnagel — **Esperanza HS, Anaheim, CA**

Pineapple-Shrimp Won Ton Cups

Makes about 3 dozen

1 package won ton skins
8 ounces cream cheese
2 tablespoons mayonnaise
1/4 cup crushed pineapple
celery salt, to taste
baby shrimp

Preheat oven to 375 degrees. Lightly oil muffin cups. Shape won ton skins to fit miniature muffin cups. Bake for 5 -7 minutes or until lightly browned. Combine cream cheese, mayonnaise, crushed pineapple, and celery salt. Fill each cup with about 1 1/2 teaspoons of filling. Top with baby shrimp.

Cups may be made ahead and frozen for several weeks. Also good with your favorite chicken salad recipe.

Sue Hope **Lompoc HS, Lompoc, CA**

Scallop Ceviche

Serves 4

12 medium size scallops
1/2 cup red onion, minced
2 scallions, minced
4 lemons, juice only
1 orange, juice only
1 tablespoon garlic, minced
1 tablespoon shallot, minced
1 bunch cilantro leaves only, chopped
1 teaspoon black pepper

Clean the scallops and set aside. Combine the onion, scallions, fruit juices, garlic, shallot, cilantro, and pepper. Add the scallops and toss to mix, cover with plastic wrap and refrigerate for 36 hours. Serve cold.

Serve this in a fancy glass such as a rarely used martini glass. This is low cal and excellent served before a spinach salad.

Yolanda Carlos **Victor Valley HS, Victorville, CA**

Shrimp Spread

Serves 4-6

1 (8 ounce) package light cream cheese
1/2 cup light sour cream
1/4 cup light mayonnaise
1 cup seafood cocktail sauce
2 cups (8 ounces) light mozzarella cheese, shredded
2 (4 1/4 ounce) cans shrimp, rinsed and drained
3 green onions, sliced
3/4 cup tomato, finely chopped
crackers, your choice

In a small bowl, beat the cream cheese, sour cream and mayonnaise until smooth. Spread on a large, round serving platter. Cover with seafood sauce. Sprinkle with cheese, shrimp, onions, and tomato. Cover and chill. Line tasty crackers around perimeter of plate.

This colorful and tasty appetizer is always a crowd pleaser. People will never know you've used lighter ingredients.

Janis Schulenburg **Irvine HS, Irvine, CA**

Sonoma Chevre with Tri-roasted Peppers

Serves 6-8

8 ounce log of good Sonoma County Goat Cheese, like Laura Chanel or Redwood Hill
1 red bell pepper
1 yellow bell pepper
1 orange bell pepper
3 tablespoons olive oil, divided
1 sprig fresh rosemary (about 1 tablespoon)
2 baguettes, sliced into 24 slices each

Place cheese log in the center of a large flat platter; cover and refrigerate. Slice the bell pepper into thin strips vertically. Heat a sauté pan over medium high heat and add 2 tablespoons of oil. Stir fry the bell peppers until they are limp, but not browned (about 7 minutes). Remove rosemary from the stem. Chop rosemary coarsely. Add to the sauté pan. Cook for one additional minute, to just release the essence of the rosemary. Remove the peppers. Toss with the 1 remaining tablespoon of olive oil. Drape the peppers over the cheese. Place the baguette slices all around the edge of the platter. Insert knife in cheese, garnish with Rosemary sprigs. Serve immediately or make ahead and chill several hours.

Excellent with a nice dry chardonnay. Refreshing on a hot afternoon, if everything is chilled down.

Marie Ganister **Windsor HS, Windsor, CA**

Spicy Chex Mix

Makes 6 quarts

1/2 box Rice Chex
1/2 box Corn Chex
1/2 box Wheat Chex
1/2 box Cheerios
1/2 bag pretzels
1/2 can mixed nuts
Spicy Seasoning Mix:
3/4 cup butter, melted
1 teaspoon Cayenne pepper
1 tablespoon garlic salt
1 teaspoon onion salt

Preheat oven to 300 degrees. Place all cereals into large baking pan; mix together. Prepare seasoning mix. Melt butter in small saucepan; add cayenne

pepper, garlic salt and onion salt; mix well. Stir while pouring seasoning mixture over cereal. Toss mixture until well coated. Bake for 45 minutes. Toss halfway through baking. Add pretzels and nuts. Cool completely before packaging.

Great gift recipe from Cindy. Just wrap in cellophane bags and add a bow.

Reiko Ikkanda — **South Pasadena MS, South Pasadena, CA**

Spinach Leaf Surprise

Makes about 35

1 package Carr's Table Water Crackers
1 medium fresh spinach leaf per cracker, remove stems
1/2 container Costco Artichoke/Jalepeno Dip, or shrimp or crab dip

Place crackers on 1 or 2 trays in a single layer; top with a spinach leaf. Place 1 teaspoonful of dip (your choice) on top of spinach leaf. *Pretty and tasty!*

Gail McAuley — **Lincoln HS, Stockton, CA**

Vegetarian Delight

Makes 15-20 pieces

1 package Crescent Rolls
2 cups vegetables, (your favorite), chopped
1(8 ounce) package cream cheese, (you may use a flavored version)

Preheat oven to the temperature on the crescent roll package. Unroll the crescent rolls and place on a cookie sheet pressing as a single layer. Bake the crescent roll layer for the time indicated on the package. Chop vegetables. When the dough is finished cooking; layer the dough with the cheese and the vegetables. Best if chilled for at least 30 minutes. Slice and serve

I love to use colorful vegetables and a garlic favored cheese for parties!

Renee Araujo — **Huntington Beach HS, Huntington Beach, CA**

Apple Goop

Serves 10

10 large apples, firm
Fresh Fruit produce protector
3 Skor bars
1 (16 ounce) container caramel dip
1 (12 ounce) brick cream cheese, softened

Use an apple wedger to core and slice apples. Place apples in a large bowl. Sprinkle generously with Fruit Fresh; toss to prevent apples from browning. Cover and refrigerate. Use a rolling pin to crush Skor bars between two sheets of waxed paper; set aside. Use an electric mixer to blend caramel with cream cheese until smooth. Mound caramel mixture in the center of a large platter. Sprinkle crushed Skor bars on top. Arrange apple slices around the caramel, and you are ready for dipping.

Thanks to my daughter, Audra, for sharing this recipe when I was in need of a delicious, quick idea. Green and red apples are perfect for the winter holidays.

Gerry Henderson — **Temple City HS, Temple City, CA**

Hot Appetizers

Avocado Mango Bruschetta

Makes 18

18 ciabatta dinner rolls or 1 baguette
2 tablespoons olive oil, divided
1 ripe, firm avocado, peeled and diced
1 cup mango, diced
1/4 cup red bell pepper, diced
2 tablespoons fresh basil, snipped
1 tablespoon lime juice
salt and freshly ground pepper, to taste

Preheat oven to 400 degrees. Place bread slices on a baking sheet and brush with 1 tablespoon olive oil. Bake for 5 minutes to lightly toast. In a large bowl, lightly stir together remaining oil with all ingredients, being careful to not mash avocado. Serve with toasted bread slices.

CTE Department stamp of approval; colorful and tasty.

Betty Plooy **Vanden HS, Fairfield, CA**

Bacon Wrap Dates

Serves 10-12

4 packages bacon
2 (10 ounce) packages pitted dates
1 (10 ounce) can Planters Almonds
1 box toothpicks

Preheat oven to 350 degrees. Cut bacon in half. Lay bacon out on a sheet pan and bake until half cooked. Remove and let cool. Stuff each date with an almond. Wrap each date in bacon and secure with a toothpick. Bake on a wire rack, until bacon is done.

Joy Sweeney Aiello **Porterville HS, Porterville, CA**

Baked Brie in Puff Pastry

Makes 20

1 round of Brie Cheese, do not remove skin
1 sheet of frozen puff pastry
4 tablespoons preserves of your choice, apricot is great
1/2 cup pecans, roughly chopped

Preheat oven to 400 degrees and prepare a baking sheet with parchment paper or nonstick cooking spray. Thaw puff pastry and bring to room temperature; roll out lightly to make the sheet large enough to cover the round of Brie and set aside. Spread the preserves and sprinkle the nuts on top of the cheese. Center the sheet of pastry on top the the round; fold all of the sides under to completely enclose the cheese. Place the Brie on the prepared baking sheet and bake for 25 minutes. Bake until puff pastry is lightly browned all over and cheese is very soft when tested in the center with a knife. Serve on a large platter with spreaders and crackers or sliced, toasted baguette.

Patty Stroming **Mitchell Sr. Elementary, Atwater, CA**

Barbequed Meatballs

Makes about 50 meatballs

2 pounds lean ground beef
2 teaspoons Worcestershire sauce
2/3 cup evaporated milk
1 envelope dry onion soup mix
Sauce:
2 cups ketchup
3/4 cup brown sugar, packed
1 tablespoon Worcestershire sauce

Mix beef, 2 teaspoons Worcestershire sauce, evaporated milk and soup mix. Shape into balls the size of walnuts. Broil 4 inches from broiler for 12 minutes, or until meatballs are browned and cooked through. Turn several times to prevent burning. Mix sauce ingredients and bring to a boil; simmer for 10 minutes. Set slow cooker on low; add meatballs and pour sauce over. Makes about 50 meatballs.

This recipe is one of our requested items for catering.

Amy Lee **Sierra HS, Manteca, CA**

Best Taco Bake

Serves 6-12

3/4 pound ground beef
2 tablespoons taco seasoning
1/3 cup water
1 tablespoon Crisco shortening
1/2 large can refried beans
1/4 cup taco sauce
3/4 cup chunky salsa
1/2 cup sour cream
2 cups cheddar and Monterey Jack cheese, grated

Preheat oven to 350 degrees. Brown ground beef in 10 inch skillet; drain fat. Add taco seasoning and water; bring to a quick boil and then let simmer for 5 minutes. Meanwhile, put shortening in bottom of small saucepan and melt on medium heat; add beans and warm until smooth. Spread refried beans in the bottom of a 9 inch deep dish pie pan. Spread taco meat evenly over refried beans. Spread taco sauce evenly over taco meat. Combine salsa and sour cream and evenly spread over top of taco sauce. Sprinkle combined cheeses evenly on top. Bake until cheese is melted. Serve with tortilla chips.

One of my students' favorites! The idea of hot sour cream does not appeal to them initially, but it makes this dip different and delicious!

Beckie Bloemker — **Foothill HS, Sacramento, CA**

Chai Tea Mix

Serves 4

1/2 cup nonfat dry milk
1/4 cup vanilla-flavored instant creamer (dry)
3 tablespoons powdered sugar
1/4 cup unsweetened instant tea (dry)
1 teaspoon ground cinnamon
1/2 teaspoon ground cardamom
1/2 teaspoon ground cloves

Combine all ingredients. Store in a glass jar. To prepare tea, spoon 3 to 4 heaping teaspoons of mix for each serving in mug and fill with 1 cup very hot water. For a creamier chai, use half milk and half water.

Makes a nice gift packaged in a mug or an attractive jar. For a fancier layered look, mix the dry milk, creamer and sugar in one bowl and the remaining ingredients in another; then spoon them alternately into a jar.

Linda Vincent — **Turlock HS, Turlock, CA**

Cheese & Green Chiles Squares

Serves 8-10

2 (4 ounce) cans mild chiles, cut into strips
3 cups Monterey Jack cheese, grated
1 1/2 cups sharp cheddar cheese, grated
2 eggs
2 tablespoons milk
1 tablespoon flour

Preheat oven to 375 degrees. In a lightly greased 9 inch square pan, layer chiles and cheese starting and ending with cheese. Beat eggs, milk, and flour; pour over layers and bake for about an hour or until firm. Allow to sit a few minutes before cutting into small squares; serve warm.

Easy to make.

Susan Lefler **Ramona HS, Chino, CA**

Cheese French Bread

Serves 12-15

1 loaf round sourdough bread, uncut
1 pound Monterey Jack cheese, sliced
2 cups butter
2 tablespoons Dijon mustard
2 teaspoons Beau Monde
2 tablespoons lemon juice

Preheat oven to 350 degrees. Vertically slice 1-inch strips from the center of the bread to 1/2-inch from the bottom of the loaf. It is important to leave the bottom uncut to hold the bread together. While keeping the shape of the loaf, carefully slice bread horizontally into 1-inch intervals making 1-inch squares down each previously sliced strip. Place entire loaf onto a baking sheet. I use my pizza stone, but a cookie sheet will work also. Slice cheese into 1-inch strips and tuck into the bread between the sides of the 1-inch squares. It's OK if the cheese sticks out the top a little. Melt the butter. Add the mustard, beau monde and lemon juice. Stir until mustard melts, too. Pour over the bread and cheese slices. Bake for 30 minutes until all the cheese melts. Serve warm. Bread squares can be pulled easily off and enjoyed.

This is very different. Tried and true and ALWAYS a hit!

Robin Butterfield **Rio Vista MS, Fresno, CA**

Cheesy Crab Squares

Makes 2 dozen

2 (8 ounce) cans refrigerated crescent dinner rolls
1/2 cup salad dressing
2 teaspoons lemon juice
1/8 teaspoon pepper
2 cups sharp cheddar cheese, shredded
6 ounces imitation crab meat, chopped
1/3 cup green onion, sliced
1 tablespoon parsley, chopped

Unroll dough into four rectangles. Place in 15 x 10 x 1 jelly roll pan; press onto bottom and halfway up sides of pan to form crust. Seal perforations. Bake at 375 degrees for 10 minutes. Combine salad dressing, juice and pepper. Mix well. Add cheese, crab meat, onions and parsley; mix lightly. Spread over crust; continue baking 12-15 minutes or until cheese is melted. Let stand 5 minutes; cut into squares. Make ahead: Prepare crust as directed; cool; cover tightly. Combine crab meat mixture as directed; cover, and chill. Spread crab meat mixture over crust just before baking. Bake at 350 degrees for 15 minutes or until cheese is melted.

May use light or low fat salad dressing and cheese to lower fat. I change the recipe by eliminating the crab meat mixture. Scatter baked crust with with fresh grated carrots, zucchini, diced red pepper. Top the veggies with freshly grated cheese.

Nina Hanna **Grace Davis HS, Modesto, CA**

Cheesy Pigs-in-the-Blanket

Makes 32

2 packages refrigerator crescent rolls
1 (8 ounce) package shredded cheddar cheese
1 (16 ounce) package little smokie links

Preheat oven to 375 degrees. Open crescent rolls, and separate triangles. Cut each triangle in half (center corner straight down to center of longer side), forming two smaller triangles. Lay triangles flat and place 1 teaspoon of cheese on each triangle, gently spread and press cheese into dough. Then, place one little smokie link on the dough near the longest edge of triangle. Roll link toward corner, wrap side corners around edges, pinching seams together to seal. Place seam side down on an ungreased cookie sheet. Bake for 20-23 minutes, until golden.

Sue Rheinwald **Spring Valley HS, Las Vegas, NV**

Chicken Satay with Peanut Sauce

Serves 6-12

1/3 cup soy sauce
1/3 cup brown sugar
2 teaspoons lime zest
1/4 cup lime juice
3 cloves garlic
1 1/2 pounds chicken breast, boneless skinless
1/3 cup creamy peanut butter
1 tablespoon cilantro, snipped

Preheat oven to 400 degrees. Combine soy sauce, brown sugar, lime zest, and lime juice. Press garlic into soy sauce mixture and mix well. Reserve 1/3 cup soy sauce mix for peanut sauce. Cut chicken into 1 inch pieces; add to remaining soy sauce mixture. Cover and marinate in refrigerator for 30 minutes. Place chicken in 9 inch baking pan. Bake for 18-20 minutes. Meanwhile, prepare peanut sauce by adding peanut butter and cilantro to 1/3 cup reserved soy sauce mixture. Whisk until smooth and serve with chicken.

Fabulous as an appetizer or as a main dish served with rice and other sides.

Teresa Hayes **Buena HS, Ventura, CA**

Chipotle Chicken Quesadillas

Makes 4 quesadillas

1 canned chipotle chile in adobo sauce, drained and minced
1/4 cup sour cream
1/4 cup mayonnaise
1 tablespoon fresh lime juice
1 tablespoon fresh cilantro
8 corn tortillas
2-3 cups cooked chicken, chopped or shredded
2 cups Monterey jack cheese, grated
Salsa

Heat grill pan, skillet or barbecue (medium heat). In small bowl, whisk together chile, sour cream, mayonnaise, lime juice, and cilantro. Spread 1 tablespoon of chile-lime sauce on each of the tortillas. Top 4 of the tortillas with the chicken and cheese, dividing each evenly, then cover with remaining 4 tortillas. Place one filled quesadilla on a plate and use the plate to help slide the quesadilla onto the pan or barbecue. Cook each quesadilla about 2 minutes on each side or until cheese is melted and tortilla is golden. Keep warm in oven until all are grilled. Slice each quesadilla in wedges and serve with salsa.

A wide spatula makes for easier turning of the quesadillas.

Laura de la Motte **Turlock HS, Turlock, CA**

Chipotle Chicken Tostadas

Serves 6-10

3 flour tortillas
1 can of spray canola oil
1 avocado
1 cup sour cream
2-3 roma tomatoes, seeded and chopped
1 tablespoon fresh lime juice
2 cups chicken, shredded
3/4 cup ketchup
1 cup brown sugar
1 tablespoon apple cider vinegar
1 tablespoon Worcestershire Sauce
1 tablespoon chili powder
1-2 tablespoons chili paste
lime zest, for garnish
cilantro, for garnish

Preheat oven to 425 degrees. Coat tortillas with spray on both sides. Cut tortilla into 1/8's. Place each piece into muffin pan slots with the corners pointing up in order to create a triangular bowl look. Bake 6-8 minutes or until they are golden brown around the majority of the chips. Put the mashed avocado meat into a bowl and mix with sour cream, tomatoes and lime juice. Place the guacamole in fridge. To make shredded chicken, boil 2 breasts in water until cooked and tender; then peel apart at the fibers with hands until you have 2 cups worth. Combine chicken with ketchup, brown sugar, apple cider vinegar, Worcestershire sauce, chili powder and chili paste in a medium saucepan and cook on medium heat for 3-5 minutes, stirring frequently. When finished, place some guacamole in bottom of tortilla chip then top with chicken mixture. Garnish with lime zest, sour cream and cilantro.

You can substitute the chili paste with 2 tablespoons of diced chipotles in adobe sauce.

Restaurant Career's Class — **Del Oro HS, Loomis, CA**

Crab Appetizer

Serves 10

1 package English muffins
1 cup mayonnaise
1/2 cup Parmesan cheese
4 skinny onions (approximately)
1/4 cup green onion, finely chopped
1 (6 ounce) can crab or shrimp

Split muffins and flatten. Day before, mix remaining ingredients and set aside. Day of, spread mixture on muffins and toast under broiler until bubbly.

Ann Taylor — **Silverado HS, Las Vegas, NV**

Crab Meat Appetizers

Makes 32

1 (7 1/2 ounces) can crab meat
1 cup Swiss cheese, grated
2 tablespoons green onion, chopped
1/2 teaspoon curry
1 cup mayonnaise
2 teaspoons lemon juice
dash Cayenne pepper,
water chestnuts, sliced
2 packages Pillsbury butter flake dinner rolls

Preheat oven to 400 degrees. Combine all ingredients, except dinner rolls and water chestnuts, in a bowl. Mix thoroughly. Pull dinner rolls apart into two pieces each. Top each piece with some of the crab mixture then top with a slice or two of water chestnut. Bake for 8 minutes on a cookie sheet.

These can be made ahead and baked just before serving. They will be eaten quickly!

Patricia Johnson — **Iron Horse MS, San Ramon, CA**

Crab Puffs

Serves 10-12

1 (8 ounce) package cream cheese
1 pound imitation crab
1 package wonton wraps

Mix the crab meat and cream cheese together until blended. Place a small amount of the mixture into the center of a wonton wrap. Pinch the corners of the wonton wrap together. Deep fry in oil until lightly browned.

This is a yummy treat that's best served warm.

Angie Ford — **Linden HS, Linden, CA**

Crab Stuffed Mushrooms

Serves 12

24 medium sized mushrooms
1/2 pound imitation crab
1/3 cup black olives, finely chopped
1/4 cup mayonnaise
2 tablespoons parsley, chopped
2 teaspoons lemon juice
1/4 teaspoon garlic powder
1/4 teaspoon onion powder
Parmesan cheese, grated

Preheat oven to 400 degrees. Remove stems from mushrooms; mince stems. In a bowl, flake crab; add minced mushroom stems, olives, mayonnaise, parsley, lemon juice, and garlic and onion powders. Fill mushroom caps with crab mixture. Sprinkle with desired amount of cheese. Place on baking sheets. Cover

with foil and bake for 12-15 minutes. Uncover and continue baking until golden brown, about 5 more minutes. Serve immediately.

This is always a popular appetizer to make and serve warm.
My family always asks for them, especially my nephews.

Carol Bridges **Mae Hensley JHS, Modesto, CA**

Crab Tartlets

Makes 60 tarts

2 large eggs
2 tablespoons all-purpose flour
1/2 cup salad dressing or mayonnaise
1/2 cup milk
3 green onions, finely chopped
1 (4 1/4 ounce) can of crab meat, drained and cartilage removed, flaked
2 cups Swiss cheese, grated
mini-tart shells, frozen, thawed

Preheat oven to 350 degrees. Beat eggs in medium bowl until frothy. Add flour, salad dressing, and milk; stir well. Add green onions, crab and cheese; stir to combine well. Place tart shells on ungreased baking sheet. Divide cheese mixture evenly among tart shells. Bake on lowest rack in oven for about 40 minutes until set.

I have served this for parties, and it has always been a hit!

Nancy Patten **Placerita JHS, Newhall, CA**

Cranberry-Brie Bites

Makes 24

1 puff pastry sheet
1 brie triangle, chilled
1 1/2 cups whole berry cranberry sauce

Preheat oven to 375 degrees. Thaw puff pastry sheet flat. Cut puff pastry sheet into 3 inch squares, and press them into greased mini muffin tins. Place a one inch slice of brie in the center of each puff pastry, and then top with one tablespoon of cranberry sauce. Bake 10 minutes, or until puff pastry corners are toasted light brown. Let cool a few minutes before serving.

Nice, quick and simple appetizer for the Holidays. One of my daughter's favorites.
Use a silicone mini-muffin pan for easy clean up.

Charlene Nugent **Petaluma JHS, Petaluma, CA**

David's Thai Spring Rolls & Sauce

Serves 10-12

Spring Roll:
1/4 cup cooking oil
1/2 pound ground turkey, (optional)
1/2 cup onion, finely chopped
1/2 cup carrot, finely chopped or shredded
1 teaspoon garlic salt
1 1/2 tablespoons soy sauce
3 cups cabbage, finely sliced
1 cup bean sprouts
1 package egg roll wraps
Sauce:
1 cup sugar
1/2 cup red wine vinegar
1/4 cup water
2 teaspoons garlic salt
2 tablespoons ketchup
1/2 teaspoon dried hot pepper, optional

Spring Roll: Heat oil in a fry pan or wok; add the next four ingredients until the meat is browned. Add soy sauce and the remaining ingredients. Let cool before wrapping in the egg roll wrap. Deep fry in approximately 1 cup of oil until light brown; drain on a paper towel. *Sauce:* Combine all ingredients in a saucepan and bring to a boil; turn to low and let cook for 5 minutes.

The students love this one! Every year new students come back asking if they get to make the egg rolls. You can modify the recipe by adding shrimp or ground chicken instead of the ground turkey.

Jeanette Neese **Enterprise HS, Redding, CA**

Deep-Fried Gyoza

Makes about 20-40

1 tablespoon canola oil
1 small onion, diced
1 tablespoon fresh ginger, minced
1 pound ground beef
3 garlic cloves, minced
1 teaspoon salt
2 teaspoons pepper
1 egg
3 green onions, finely sliced
1 package of won-ton wraps
4 inches of vegetable oil (depending on size of pan) for deep frying

Put 1 tablespoon of canola oil in a large sauté pan over medium high heat. Add diced onion; sauté until translucent. Add fresh ginger; stir. Add ground beef; stir. While mixture is browning, add minced garlic, salt, and pepper. After meat is browned, drain and set aside for about 5 minutes to cool. Add 1 egg and green onion; stir. Place 1 tablespoon of beef mixture in middle of a wonton wrap. Wet

finger with water and dampen the edges of wonton wrap. Gently fold wonton to seal the beef mixture. Be sure to carefully pinch out any air bubbles to prevent breakage or popping while frying. Do not stack prepped gyoza. In a deep-frying pan, heat vegetable oil to about 375 degrees. Depending on size of pan, deep fry gyoza until golden brown. Do not over crowd pan. If gyoza browns instantly, turn down heat. When golden brown, remove from oil and place on wire mesh or metal cooling rack (preferably gyozas placed vertically) to drain excess oil before resting on paper towels. Serve immediately; best served crisp.

This is my mother's personalized gyoza recipe. Her gyoza is always a huge hit at potluck gatherings. Easy, delicious and versatile. Filling can vary according to your taste. For a healthier option, steam gyoza instead of deep-fry.

Miho Hosaka — **North Eugene HS, Eugene, OR**

Double Trouble Bruschetta

Makes 12

6 roma (plum) tomatoes, chopped
1/2 cup sun-dried tomatoes, packed in oil, chopped
3 cloves garlic, minced
1/4 cup olive oil
2 tablespoons balsamic vinegar
1/4 cup fresh basil, stems removed and chiffonade
1/4 teaspoon salt
1/4 teaspoon ground black pepper
1 French baguette
1 cup mozzarella cheese, shredded
1/4 cup Parmesan cheese, shredded

In a large bowl, combine the roma tomatoes, sun-dried tomatoes, garlic, olive oil, balsamic vinegar, basil, salt, and pepper. Allow the mixture to sit for 10 minutes. Now, preheat oven on LOW broiler setting. Cut the baguette into 3/4 inch hard diagonal slices. On a baking sheet, arrange the baguette slices in a single layer. Broil for 1 to 2 minutes, until slightly brown. Divide the tomato mixture evenly over the baguette slices. Top the slices with a mixture of both cheeses. Broil on MIDDLE rack for 3-5 minutes, or until the cheese is melted. Remove from oven, let set. Let the party begin!

Make it for all your parties...it is a hit for even the snobbiest guests!!

Alan von der Mehden — **Pleasant Valley HS, Chico, CA**

Easy Stuffed Mussrooms

Serves 20-24

3 pounds(approximately) large fresh mushrooms
1 (8 ounce) block cream cheese
1 (16 ounce) roll Jimmy Dean Spicy Sausage

Wash, remove stems and pat dry mushroom caps. Set aside. Let cream cheese soften at room temperature in mixing bowl while frying sausage until thoroughly cooked and in small crumbly pieces. Drain fat, then press between paper towels and remove excess grease. Stir sausage into cream cheese and blend well. Fill

mushroom caps with mixture by rounded spoonfuls, then place on foil lined cookie sheets. Place under broiler for a few minutes until mushrooms soften and cheese mixture is bubbly. Remove to serving platter and enjoy!

Every time we serve these, someone wants the recipe. So easy and delicious!

Carol Winter — **Copper Hills HS, West Jordon, UT**

Fried Crab Won Tons with Sweet & Sour Sauce

Serves 6

4 ounces cream cheese
1-2 green onions, finely chopped
1/8 pound imitation crab
1/2 package Won Ton wrappers
Sweet & Sour Sauce:
3/4 cup pineapple juice
2/3 cup golden brown sugar
2 tablespoons vinegar
1/2 teaspoon soy sauce
2 teaspoons ketchup
2 tablespoons cornstarch

Won tons: In a medium bowl mash cream cheese till smooth. Add green onions and imitation crab and mix until uniform consistency. Fill won tons with 1/2 teaspoon of mixture. Place water around edges of won tons, so when folded they stay together. Heat oil in wok on medium heat. Deep fry won tons until golden brown. Place on paper towels to cool. Dip in your favorite sauce. Serve. *Sweet & Sour Sauce:* Put all ingredients into bowl and mix until blended. Place ingredients in a small saucepan and heat on the stovetop until sauce has thickened. Adjust flavor if needed.

My students love this delicious recipe.
They especially love it with the sweet and sour sauce.

Susie McGuire — **Woodcreek HS, Roseville, CA**

Fried Green Tomatoes

Serves 4-8

1/2 cup cornmeal
1/2 cup flour
2 tablespoons garlic salt
2 teaspoons cayenne pepper
2 teaspoons Trader Joe's 21 Seasoning Salute
2 tablespoons milk
3 eggs
2 green tomatoes
2 cups canola oil, for frying

Mix dry ingredients into a shallow bowl. In another bowl mix milk and eggs together. Wash and slice green tomatoes, thinly. Heat oil, until hot enough to fry (by testing a small amount of flour into oil). Dip green tomato into egg batter,

then into flour mixture. Note: Tomato is better, if you double dip it! Fry until golden brown and drain on paper towels. Serve hot with ranch dressing dip.

You can have this along with the movie one evening! A fun treat to have anytime!

Donna Abbey — **Central MS, Oroville, CA**

Fried Won Tons

Makes 15 Won Tons

1/4 lb. ground pork
3 water chestnuts, finely chopped
1 1/2 teaspoons soy sauce
1/2 teaspoon cornstarch
1/4 teaspoon salt
1/2 pound won ton skins
sweet and sour sauce

In a frying pan cook the pork, breaking it into small pieces. Mix together pork, chestnuts, soy sauce, cornstarch and salt. Place one teaspoon of the pork mixture on the center of a won ton skin. Moisten the edges of the won ton skin with water. Fold each skin in half to form a triangle and press edges to seal. Heat 1 inch of oil to 360 degrees. Fry six won tons at a time until golden brown. Turn occasionally. Drain on paper towels. Serve with sweet and sour sauce.

Debbie Harvey — **Amador Valley HS, Pleasanton, CA**

Gouda Puff

Makes 16

1 round of gouda cheese
2 packages refrigerated crescent rolls
1 egg, beaten

Cut gouda cheese through the center so that you have two round pieces. Separate triangles of rolls and make two circles with them sealing edges. Place cheese in center of each circle and bring dough over the top of the cheese overlapping the pieces so that the cheese is completely sealed inside. Brush with egg and cook at temperature on refrigerated roll package until puffed and golden brown.

Looks like a lot of work, but very simple and delicious!

Linda Woolley — **Redlands HS, Redlands, CA**

Gouda-Stuffed Mushrooms

Serves 8

6 ounces Pancetta (Italian bacon) or Canadian bacon, finely diced
2 tablespoons butter
1 small onion, finely diced
3 cloves garlic, minced
2 cups Gouda cheese, shredded
3/4 cup fresh breadcrumbs
2 tablespoons fresh basil, chopped
Kosher salt and freshly ground black pepper, to taste
24 (2 inch) Crimini mushroom caps

Preheat oven to 400 degrees. In a medium skillet, sauté Pancetta or Canadian bacon over medium-high heat until crisp, about 3 minutes. Remove to mixing bowl; discard fat from skillet. Melt butter in same skillet over medium heat. Add onion and garlic; sauté 3 minutes. Stir in cheese, breadcrumbs, and basil. Season with Kosher salt and pepper. Place mushroom caps on baking sheet. Mound about 2 1/2 tablespoons cheese mixture into center of each mushroom cap. Bake 8 minutes. Serve hot. You may add 1 cup of fresh spinach, packed and chopped after you sauté the onion and garlic. Stir in the spinach; cook until wilted. Add the Pancetta and allow to cool slightly. Then stir in the cheese, breadcrumbs, and basil.

Kathie Baczynski — **Mt. Carmel HS, Poway, CA**

Ham & Swiss Pinwheels

Makes 16

2 teaspoons all purpose flour
1 (1 pound) loaf frozen white bread dough, thawed
3 tablespoons Dijon mustard
1 tablespoon honey
2 cups reduced-fat Swiss cheese, shredded
4 (1 ounce) slices lean, cooked turkey ham
2 tablespoons pepperoncini, drained and chopped
vegetable cooking spray

Preheat oven to 350 degrees. Sprinkle flour evenly over clean work surface. Turn dough onto floured surface and roll to a 12 inch square. Combine mustard and honey in a small bowl; brush mixture over dough. Sprinkle rolled dough evenly with cheese; top with ham slices. Sprinkle with pepperoncini. Roll up dough, jelly roll fashion; pinch seam to seal. (Do not seal ends.) Cut roll into 16 slices. Place slices, cut side down, on a baking sheet coated with cooking spray. Cover with a damp cloth and let rise in a warm place (75-85 degrees), free from drafts for 45 minutes. Bake for 15-18 minutes or until golden brown. Serve immediately.

135 calories; 4.3 fat

Dee Ann Verdi — **McQueen HS, Reno, NV**

Prosciutto & Wisconsin Fontina Cheese Fritters

Serves 8

Fondue:
5 plum tomatoes
2 cloves garlic, minced
2 tablespoons onion, finely diced
1 to 2 tablespoons olive oil
1 to 2 teaspoons hot smoked Spanish paprika
salt & pepper to taste

Fritters:
2 cups Wisconsin Fontina cheese, grated
1/4 cups prosciutto ham, dices
2 tablespoons all-purpose flour
1/4 teaspoon fresh rosemary, chopped
2 tablespoons whole milk
1 egg, lightly beaten
2 cups Panko Japenese bread crumbs
1 gallon peanut or grape seed oil

Fondue: Char tomatoes until blistered and dark, 5 to 8 minutes. Remove seeds, dice and skin. Cook garlic and onion in olive oil until tender. Add paprika and heat for 1 minute. Add tomatoes; season with salt and pepper. Keep warm. *Fritters:* In large bowl, combine cheese and ham. Toss with flour. Add rosemary. Fold in milk and egg. Form 24 quarter-sized patties, using level tablespoon. Coat patties with bread crumbs. Heat oil to 350 to 375 degrees in deep fryer. Fry in batches until golden brown, about 30 seconds.

Recipes and photos courtesy of Wisconsin Milk Marketing Board

Braised Stuffed Artichokes

Makes 6

2 1/2 cups cubed day-old Italian bread, crust removed, or 2 cups bread crumbs
1 egg
4 ounces Wisconsin Pleasant Ridge Reserve cheese, small cubes
2 tablespoons grated Wisconsin Stravecchio cheese
juice of 1 lemon
6 fresh artichokes
24 pearl onions, peeled
12 roasted garlic cloves
3 anchovy filets
1/4 cup olive oil
1 cup white wine
salt and pepper

Pre-heat oven to 375 degrees. Stuffing: Process bread in food processor, or use prepared crumbs. Place 2 cups into large bowl. Add egg and toss to coat. Stir in both cheeses. Set aside. Artichokes: Add lemon juice to pot of water. Trim stem and outer rows of leaves from artichokes. Dip artichokes in lemon water often to prevent oxidation. Cut off top 1/4 of artichoke. Scoop out interior, including the fuzzy choke. Dry artichokes well. Stuff with cheese mixture. Place stuffed artichokes, stems up, in large oiled baking dish. Add onions, garlic and anchovies to baking dish. Drizzle with olive oil and wine. Cover dish with aluminum foil. Bake 45 minutes or until artichokes are tender, turning stem side down after 25 minutes. Place artichokes on one large serving plate. Drizzle sauce, decorate the plate with onions and garlic.

Prosciutto & Wisconsin Fontina Cheese Fritters

Braised Stuffed Artichokes

Bacon, Lettuce
& Tomato Bruschetta

Bacon, Lettuce & Tomato Bruschetta

Makes 24

8-10 slices bacon, crispy cooked and crumbled
3-4 Roma (plum) tomatoes, seeded
and chopped (about 1 1/3 cup)
1 cup chopped leafy green lettuce
2 tablespoons chopped fresh basil leaves
1 clove garlic, minced
1/4 teaspoon salt
1/4 teaspoon ground pepper
Approximately 1/3 cup olive oil
1/2 package (16-oz.) twin French bread loaves,
cut in 1/4 -inch slices
1/3 cup favorite crumble cheese, blue cheese or feta (optional)

In medium bowl, stir together all topping ingredients; set aside. Brush olive oil on both sides of bread slices; place on baking sheet. Bake at 400 degrees F., turning once, for 7 minutes per side or until crisp and golden brown; cool. Spoon about 1 tablespoon topping on each toast round. Makes about 24 appetizers. Or, serve topping in a small bowl, surrounded by the toast rounds. *Tailgate Tip:* Prepare and refrigerate topping ingredients and bake toast rounds ahead of time. For best flavor, stir together topping ingredients just before serving.

Recipe and photo courtesy of National Pork Board

Hot Seafood Spread

Makes 4 cups

8 ounces cream cheese
2 cups cheddar cheese, shredded
1 cup mayonnaise
4 1/2 ounces tiny shrimp
1 cup imitation crab meat, chopped
1/2 cup green onion, chopped
1/4 cup Parmesan cheese, grated
2 teaspoons dill weed
fresh parsley, (optional)
1 (1 1/2 pounds) loaf round bread, unsliced
assorted vegetables and crackers

Preheat oven to 350 degrees. Mix all ingredients, except bread, assorted vegetables and crackers. Cut top off of bread; carefully hollow out. Cube removed bread and set aside. Fill bread with seafood mixture. Place on baking sheet; cover loosely with foil and bake for 25 minutes. Remove foil and bake 20 to 30 minutes longer until crust is golden. Serve with bread, vegetables, or crackers.

So easy to fill up on, you may not want any dinner.

Robin Ali **Nevada Union HS, Grass Valley, CA**

Italian Appetizer Bites

Makes 32

2 (8 ounce) packages refrigerated crescent rolls
1/2 pound deli salami, sliced
1/2 pound provolone cheese
1/2 pound deli ham, sliced
7 eggs
1 cup Parmesan cheese, grated
2 (12 ounce) jars roasted red peppers, drained

Preheat oven to 350 degrees. Coat a 9 x 13 baking dish with nonstick spray. Unroll 1 package crescent rolls and use dough to line the bottom of the baking dish. Pinch seams together with fingers. Cover rolls with half salami, provolone, and ham. Lightly beat together 6 of the eggs and parmesan cheese; pour half evenly over top. Top with half of the roasted red peppers. Repeat layering with remaining salami, provolone, ham, egg mixture and peppers. Top with remaining package of crescent rolls. Lightly beat remaining egg and brush over top. Cover top with foil; bake for 30 minutes. Uncover and bake 30 minutes more. Cool for 1 hour; cut into 32 squares and serve.

My sister, Pam, gave this recipe to me. She found it in a magazine and has made it many times. "Everyone loves them".

Penny Childers **Ramona HS, Ramona, CA**

Italian Chicken Nuggets

Makes 120 bite-sized pieces

20 chicken breasts, boneless, skinless, cut into chunks
6 eggs
1/2 cup milk
1 can Italian bread crumbs
2 tablespoons garlic powder
1 cube butter
1/2 cup olive oil
2 cups chicken broth
2 lemons, juiced

Preheat oven to 350 degrees. Mix egg and milk, toss with chicken. Toss in bread crumbs mixed with garlic powder. Brown pieces in melted butter and olive oil. Transfer to a large baking dish; add chicken broth and lemon juice. Bake until chicken is cooked through.

I borrowed this from a good friend, Lori Oliva. This recipe makes a great party buffet item and can be prepared ahead, frozen and reheated.

Terri Seifried — **Valencia HS, Valencia, CA**

Janice's Stuffed Mushrooms

Serves 15-20

1 (8 ounce) package cream cheese
1 1/2 jars Hormel Bacon Bits
3 boxes mushrooms, whole, bite size, no stems

Preheat oven to 350 degrees. Mix the cream cheese and bacon bits together. Stuff the mushrooms with the mixture. Place on a greased baking sheet; bake for 20 minutes.

You may want to double this recipe, because your guests will certainly devour this delicious appetizer!

Bonnie Landin — **Garden Grove HS, Garden Grove, CA**

Josefinas

Makes 3 dozen

1 baguette, regular or sourdough; be sure it is long enough to get 36 1/4 inch slices
2 cubes butter, softened
2 cloves garlic, pressed
1 small can chopped Ortega chiles
1 cup mayonnaise
2 cups Jack cheese, grated

Slice baguette into 1/4 inch slices and place on cookie sheet. Toast in broiler until slices are lightly browned. Turn toasted baguettes over to prepare for topping. In a small bowl combine the butter, garlic and chopped chiles. Spread mixture onto bread rounds. In a small bowl combine the mayonnaise and Jack cheese. Spread this mixture onto the butter mixture. At this point the Josefinas may be covered and refrigerated until ready to be served. When ready to serve:

preheat broiler and broil until Josefinas are hot, bubbly and lightly browned. Serve immediately.

These are definitely an indulgence in calories but well worth it. Serve them for a special occasion; your guests will love them!

Beth Guerrero **Selma HS, Selma, CA**

Kielbasa Bites

Serves 6-10

Polska Kielbasa sausage
1 cup red wine vinegar
1 cup brown sugar

Cut kielbasa sausage into bite size pieces. Brown in skillet until desired doneness. Pour red wine vinegar and brown sugar into skillet. Stir and continue cooking until liquid mixture is reduced to a thick syrup.

Easy and delicious. Family and friends request that this dish be brought to all our get-togethers. Usually the first appetizer to disappear from the table. Clearly a favorite!

Myra Skidmore **Downey HS, Downey, CA**

Mexican Cheese Fondue

Serves 4-6

3 tablespoons butter
3 tablespoons flour
1/8 teaspoon garlic powder
2/3 cup half and half
1/2 cup chicken broth, plus more to thin sauce if needed
1 1/2 cups Monterey Jack cheese, shredded
3 tablespoons mild salsa

Melt butter in small saucepan over medium heat. Whisk in flour and garlic powder until blended. Whisk in half and half and chicken broth. Continue to heat the mixture until it thickens and starts to bubble,about 2 minutes. Reduce heat to low. Gradually add the cheese, stirring until melted; stir in salsa. Transfer to fondue pot. Add broth, a little at a time, to achieve desired consistency.

This is a fun way to get kids to try different veggies.

Paula Skrifvars **Brea JHS, Brea, CA**

Mexican Pizza Nachos

Serves 8

1 pound chorizo (beef or pork)
1 (1 pound) bag tortilla chips
2 cups Jack cheese, grated
1 (14 ounce) can diced green chiles
sour cream, for topping

Fry chorizo; drain off grease. Arrange chips on baking sheet; top with cooked chorizo; sprinkle on cheese and green chiles. Place in broiler and heat until all of the cheese is hot and melted. Top with dollops of sour cream.

Nice change from the everyday nachos. If you like it hot, use jalapeños. Great before football games!

Wendy Duncan — **West Covina HS, West Covina, CA**

Michelle's Hot Brie

Serves 6-10

1 Brie wedge (1/4 Brie)
1/2 bottle honey mustard (any brand)
8 slices bacon, cooked and crumbled
6 green onions, chopped

Preheat oven to 350 degrees. Place Brie in a small glass baking dish; cover with honey mustard. Top with crumbled bacon and green onion. Bake, uncovered, until hot. Serve with crackers or bread.

This is my stepdaughter's favorite appetizer for any party. Now it's also my favorite.

Charlotte Runyon — **Saddleback HS, Santa Ana, CA**

Mini Tortilla Quiches

Makes 32

nonstick cooking spray
5 (10 inch) plain, spinach, or tomato flour tortillas
1 cup fresh cilantro, chopped
1/2 cup half and half or light cream
1/2 cup green onions, sliced
2 eggs
1/4 teaspoon salt
1/8 teaspoon cayenne pepper
3 tablespoons dairy sour cream
paprika

Preheat oven to 375 degrees. Lightly coat 32 (1 3/4 inch) muffin cups with nonstick cooking spray; set aside. Using a 3 inch round cutter, cut 32 circles form the tortillas; gently press one round into each muffin cup, pleating rounds as necessary to fit. Set cups aside. For filling: In a blender, combine cilantro, half and half, green onions, eggs, salt, and cayenne pepper; cover and blend until the mixture is smooth. Spoon a scant tablespoon filling into each tortilla-lined muffin cup. Bake about 15 minutes or until filling is completely set when poked near center with a wooden toothpick. Carefully remove quiches from muffin cups. Before serving, spoon 1/4 teaspoon sour cream atop each warm quiche and sprinkle with paprika.

If you have only one muffin pan, prepare the tortilla rounds and filling as directed and bake the quiches in three batches, keeping the filling chilled between batches.

Phyllis Langlois — **Green Valley HS, Las Vegas, NV**

Parmesan Twists

Makes 28

1 sheet frozen Puff pastry sheets (1/2 package)
1 egg
1 tablespoon water
1/4 cup parmesan cheese, grated
1 tablespoon fresh parsley, chopped
1/2 teaspoon oregano leaves

Preheat oven to 400 degrees. Thaw out puff pastry sheet at room temperature, about 30 min. Mix together all remaining ingredients in a bowl. Roll out the puff pastry sheet to a 14 x 10 rectangle, on a lightly floured surface; cut in half lengthwise. Brush the egg mixture onto one half of the pastry sheet. Place the other sheet on top, making a sandwich of the egg mixture. Roll slightly to seal edges and to make bigger. Cut the pastry sandwich into about 1 1/2 inch strips, twist strips and place on a parchment paper on the baking sheet. Top with additional grated parmesan, if desired. Bake 10 minutes or until golden brown.

This is a student adjusted recipe that has become quite a hit around our district.

Niki Clausen — **Reynolds HS, Troutdale, OR**

Pizza Sticks

Makes 8 breadsticks

1 tube refrigerated breadsticks
24 pepperoni slices
2 tablespoons Parmesan cheese, grated
1/2 teaspoon Italian seasoning
1/4 teaspoon garlic powder
1/2 cup pizza sauce, warmed

Preheat oven to 350 degrees. Unroll breadstick dough and separate into eight pieces. Place three pepperoni slices on the bottom half of each breadstick, leaving about 3/4 inch of dough at the end. Fold top of dough over pepperoni and pinch end to seal; twist breadsticks. Place on ungreased baking sheets. Combine the Parmesan cheese, Italian seasoning and garlic powder; sprinkle over breadsticks. Bake for 15-20 minutes or until golden brown. Serve with sauce.

Fast, easy, and so yummy!

Katrina James — **Basic HS, Henderson, NV**

Prosciutto-Wrapped Figs with Gorgonzola & Walnuts

Makes 18

9 large fresh black Mission Figs, stemmed and halved
18 (1 x 5 inch) thin strips prosciutto (about 3 ounces)
3 tablespoons Gorgonzola
18 large walnut pieces, toasted

Preheat broiler. Cover large rimmed baking sheet with foil. Wrap each fig half with 1 prosciutto strip; place on prepared sheet. Broil until prosciutto chars slightly on edges, about 1 1/2 minutes. Turn figs; broil about 1 1/2 minutes

longer, watching closely to prevent burning. Place 1/2 teaspoon Gorgonzola on top of each fig half. Top each with walnut piece. Serve warm or at room temperature.

Janet Tingley — **Atascadero HS, Atascadero, CA**

Quick Pesto Appetizers

Serves 16

1 loaf cocktail size French bread
1 jar pesto (green)
3 tomatoes, sliced
grated cheese

Preheat oven to 350 degrees. Arrange bread slices on a cookie sheet. Spread each slice with pesto. Put one slice of tomato on each bread slice. Top with grated cheese Bake until cheese is melted and appetizer is heated through. Enjoy!

The colors in this appetizer are great for a Christmas party.

Pat Peck — **Folsom HS, Folsom, CA**

Roasted Grapes & Onions

Makes 1 1/2 cups

3 cups (about 1 pound) red seedless grapes, stemmed
1 cup red onion, thinly sliced
1 tablespoon olive oil
1 tablespoon balsamic vinegar
salt

Preheat oven to 450 degrees. Rinse and drain grapes. In a 9 x 13 inch pan, mix grapes with red onion and olive oil. Bake for 40-45 minutes until grapes are browned and begin to collapse. Stir halfway through cooking time. Remove from oven and stir in balsamic vinegar and salt to taste. Scrape into a small bowl. Serve warm or at room temperature.

Try this relish on toasted slices of a French bread baguette spread with fresh chevre (goat) cheese. This is so easy and so good!

Julie Shelburne — **Tulare Union HS, Tulare, CA**

Rosemary Cream Cheese Bake

Serves 6-10

1 package crescent rolls
1 bunch fresh rosemary
1 block of cream cheese

Preheat oven to 375 degrees. Roll out crescent dough into a rectangle; do not pull them apart. Place block of cream cheese into center of the dough and sprinkle with fresh rosemary. Tie up the dough into a knot by twisting and pinching the sides of the dough. Bake for 20 minutes or until dough is golden brown. Serve warm with Wheat Thin crackers.

Easy recipe; everyone always loves it!

Tracie Priske — **West Ranch HS, Stevenson Ranch, CA**

Rumaki

Serves 6-8

1 can water chestnuts, drained
soy sauce to cover
1/4 teaspoon ground ginger
sliced bacon

Marinate the water chestnuts overnight in the soy sauce. Wrap 1/2 slice bacon around the chestnut and secure with a toothpick. Broil until the bacon is crisp. Enjoy.

Dr. Terry Kluever — **Coronado HS, Henderson, NV**

Sausage Wraps

Makes 3 dozen

1 package Little Smokies (sausage wieners)
bacon
brown sugar

Preheat oven to 400 degrees. Cut bacon strips into thirds and wrap each sausage with a third. Secure with a toothpick and place in a foil lined 9 x 13 inch pan . Cover with brown sugar and bake 15-20 minutes.

Always a big hit in our appetizer lab. Never any left over.

Carla Coyle — **Whittier HS, Whittier, CA**

Skewered Rosemary Shrimp with Mint Pesto

Makes 24

Mint Pesto:
1/2 cup pine nuts, toasted
3 cloves garlic, peeled
2 tablespoons feta cheese, packed
2 tablespoons Parmesan cheese, packed
1 tablespoon jalapeño chili, coarsely chopped
1/2 teaspoon salt
1/2 teaspoon ground black pepper
2 cups fresh mint leaves, packed
2 tablespoons fresh lemon juice
1/2 cup extra-virgin olive oil
Shrimp:
24 large (about 2 pounds) shrimp, uncooked, deveined, tails left intact
2 tablespoons olive oil
2 cloves garlic, minced
1 tablespoon fresh parsley, chopped
3 tablespoons fresh lemon juice
24 woody rosemary sprigs, or wooden skewers, 4 inches long

Mint Pesto: Combine first 7 ingredients in processor. Using on/off turns, process until mixture is smooth. Add mint leaves and lemon juice; process until smooth, stopping occasionally to scrape down sides of bowl. Gradually add oil and process until mint pesto is smooth and creamy. (Can be made 1 day ahead;

cover and refrigerate.) *Shrimp:* Preheat broiler. Sprinkle shrimp with salt and pepper. Whisk oil, garlic, and parsley in medium bowl to blend. Add shrimp; toss to coat. Let stand at room temperature 15 minutes. Arrange shrimp in single layer on broiler pan. Broil until opaque in center, about 2 minutes per side. Transfer to large bowl; sprinkle with lemon juice and toss with 1/2 cup mint pesto. The remaining pesto can be used for another dish, like pasta. Starting at base end of rosemary, skewer 1 shrimp on each sprig. Arrange on platter and serve.

This is an excellent appetizer recipe given to me by my friend, Darcy. It is well worth the effort.

Millie Deeton **Rueben S. Ayala HS, Chino Hills, CA**

"So Good" Asparagus Appetizers

Serves 10-20

20 thin slices sandwich bread, crusts removed
4 ounces blue cheese, room temperature
1 (8 ounce) package cream cheese, room temperature
1 egg, beaten
3/4 pound butter
20 fresh asparagus spears, cleaned and tuff end cut off

Trim crusts from bread and flatten slightly with a rolling pin. In a bowl, stir blue and cream cheeses together with the egg until well blended and creamy. Spread a thin layer of cheese mixture over each slice of bread. Roll one asparagus spear inside each and fasten with a toothpick. Melt butter in a small saucepan. Roll each asparagus wrap in butter to coat. Place on a baking sheet and freeze for one hour, or until butter hardens and wraps are somewhat firm. Remove pan from freezer, discard toothpicks, and cut each wrap in half crosswise. Store in a resealable plastic bag in the freezer until ready to use. To serve, preheat oven to 400 degrees. Arrange frozen asparagus wraps on an ungreased baking sheet. Bake in the preheated oven for 25 minutes or until lightly browned. Check occasionally, and turn if necessary, for even browning and to prevent burning.

These are SO GOOD! We serve them at our school restaurant and everyone always asks for more. Great to keep extras in your freezer at home and when unexpected guests drop in you just pop them in the oven. They will be so impressed!

Brenda Burke **Mt. Whitney HS, Visalia, CA**

Sopes

Makes 16

2 cups masa harina flour (Mexican corn masa mix)
1/4 cup shortening or lard
1 1/4 cups warm water
1(4 ounce) can diced green chiles
2-3 teaspoons vegetable oil
Toppings: refried beans, cheddar or Monterey Jack cheese,
sour cream, salsa, jalepeno slices, sliced olives

Place flour in large mixer bowl; cut in shortening with a pastry blender or two knives until mixture resembles course crumbs. Gradually add water, kneading dough until smooth. Add chiles; mix well. Form dough into 16 small balls; flatten to form a patty. Heat vegetable oil in medium skillet; cook patties for 2-3 minutes each side or until golden. Top sopes with desired toppings.

Guests will love topping their sopes to their liking.

Mary Keane-Gruener — **Toll MS, Glendale, CA**

Spiced Pumpkin Pie Spread

Serves 4-8

4 ounces reduced fat cream cheese
1(15 ounce) can solid pack pumpkin
1/2 cup brown sugar, firmly packed
2 teaspoons pumpkin pie spice
3/4 cup miniature marshmallows
1/4 cup pecans, coarsely chopped
2 red or green apples, cut into wedges

Preheat oven to 350 degrees. Beat the cream cheese until smooth. Add pumpkin, brown sugar, and pumpkin pie spice; mix well. Spoon mixture into an oven proof ramekin or small casserole; top with marshmallows and pecans. Bake 12 to 15 minutes or until marshmallows are light golden brown. Cut apples into wedges. Serve warm with apple wedges.

This warm appetizer spread is perfect for the cool fall parties.
It is also fun to use a combination of red and green apples around holiday time.

Barbara Henshaw — **Foothill HS, Pleasanton, CA**

Spinach & Cheese Cups

Makes 30

2 (2.1 ounce) packages frozen mini phyllo shells
1/3 cup frozen, chopped spinach
(thawed, squeezed dry, and loosely packed)
1/2 cup mozzarella cheese, shredded
1/4 cup Parmesan cheese, shredded
1/4 cup ricotta cheese
2 tablespoons prosciutto, chopped
1/4 teaspoon garlic powder

Preheat oven to 350 degrees. Place phyllo shells on a large, flat baking sheet. Stir together remaining ingredients in a medium bowl and spoon into shells. Bake for 12 to 15 minutes or until cheese is melted and tops are lightly browned.

Cindy Peters — **Deer Valley HS, Antioch, CA**

Spinach & Artichoke in Puff Pastry

Serves 6-12

1/4 cup chopped spinach, from frozen,thawed and well drained
1(14 ounce) can artichoke hearts or bottoms,
chopped into pea size pieces
1/2 cup mayonnaise
1/2 cup Parmesan cheese
1 teaspoon garlic powder
1 teaspoon onion powder
1/4 teaspoon black pepper
1 (17.3 ounce) package puff pastry dough

Preheat oven to 400 degrees. Thaw puff pastry at room temperature. Drain spinach in a colander; dry on a paper towel. In a large bowl, stir together spinach, artichokes, mayonnaise, garlic powder, onion powder, and black pepper. Cut unfolded puff pastry dough into three even parts; unfold and place on a lightly floured surface or waxed paper. Cut each unfolded strip in half. Place pastry dough on a cookie sheet; carefully drop the spinach mixture over 1/2 of the rectangle. Fold the other half over the mixture and pinch to seal edges. Bake for 20-25 minutes or until golden brown.

Doris Barela-Fossen — **Sierra Vista JHS, Canyon Country, CA**

Spinach Pita

Makes 24-30 pieces

60 ounces frozen spinach, defrosted, chopped
6 eggs
1/2 onion, finely chopped
1 cup butter, divided
1 pound feta cheese
8 ounces ricotta cheese
2 tablespoons dill weed
1/2 teaspoon salt
1/4 teaspoon white pepper
1/4 teaspoon garlic powder
1 pound phyllo

Preheat oven to 350 degrees. Squeeze all the liquid out of the spinach and place into a large bowl. Sauté the onion in one tablespoon of butter and add to the spinach mixture. Add the cheeses and the spices to the mixture and mix well. Melt the remaining butter in a small frying pan. Open the phyllo package and brush one sheet lightly with butter, fold lengthwise in 3. Brush lightly with butter. Starting at the top corner, place 2 tablespoons of the spinach mixture. Fold corner over to make a triangle and continue folding as a flag so you end up with a triangle. Place fold side down on a parchment paper covered baking sheet. Bake for 25 minutes until golden. Remove and eat warm.

Maria Nicolaides — **Oceanview HS, Huntington Beach, CA**

Stuffed Mushrooms

Serves 15-20

3 boxes mushrooms - enough for each person to have about 5
1 (8 ounce) package cream cheese (not whipped)
1 small can of diced chiles

Preheat oven to 350 degrees. Wash and dry mushrooms. Remove stems by snapping them out, leaving a well. Fill well with cream cheese. Put mushrooms in a baking dish with cream cheese side up. Top each mushroom with some diced chiles. Bake for 15 to 20 minutes. They are done when there is some juice at the bottom of the pan.

My family insists I make these for every holiday get together.

Lisa Washmuth — San Luis Obispo HS, San Luis Obispo, CA

Stuffed Olives

Serves 4-6

2 (5 ounce) jars bacon cheese spread (Kraft)
1/2 cup butter
dash hot Tabasco sauce
dash Worcestershire sauce
1 1/2 cups flour
30 green stuffed olives (about)

Preheat oven to 400 degrees. Blend cheese and butter together until light and fluffy. Add both sauces, mix well. Stir in flour to form dough. Shape about 1 teaspoon of dough around each olive. Place on ungreased baking sheet. Bake for 12-15 minutes or until lightly browned.

Can leave the olives out and just make cheese balls.

Paulette Evans — Cyprus HS, Magna, UT

Sugar Glazed Brie

Serves 15-20

1/4 cup brown sugar
1/4 cup macadamia nuts or pecans, chopped
1 tablespoon brandy
1 (14 ounce) wedge brie
4 apples, cored and cut into wedges
2-3 tablespoons lemon juice
assorted crackers

In a small bowl, stir together the sugar, nuts and brandy. Cover and chill for at least 24 hours or up to 1 week. Preheat oven to 500 degrees. Place the brie on an ovenproof platter. Bake for 4-5 minutes or until the brie is slightly softened. Spread the sugar mixture on top of the warm brie and bake again for 2-3 minutes, or until the sugar melts. Brush the apple wedges with lemon juice and arrange them around one side of the brie. Place crackers around the other side.

Great for holiday parties!

Jill Marsh — Warren HS, Downey, CA

Taco Meatball Ring

Serves 10-15

2 cups (8 ounces) shredded cheddar cheese, divided
2 tablespoons water
2 to 4 tablespoons taco seasoning
1/2 pound ground beef
2 (8 ounce) tubes refrigerated crescent rolls
1/2 head lettuce, shredded
1 medium tomato, chopped
4 green onions, sliced
1/2 cup sliced ripe olives
sour cream
salsa, optional

Combine 1 cup cheese, water and taco seasoning in a mixing bowl. Add beef and mix well; shape into 16 balls. Place 1 inch apart in an ungreased 15 x 10 baking pan. Bake, uncovered, at 400 degrees for 12 minutes or until meat is no longer pink; drain meatballs on paper towels. Reduce heat to 375 degrees. Arrange crescent rolls on a greased 15 inch pizza pan forming a ring with pointed ends facing the outer edge of the pan and wide ends overlapping. Place a meatball on each roll; fold point over meatball and tuck under wide end of roll (meatballs will be visible). Bake for 15-20 minutes or until rolls are golden brown. Fill the center of ring with lettuce, tomato, onion, olives, remaining cheese, sour cream and salsa if desired.

Diana Lee — **David A. Brown MS, Wildomar, CA**

Tempting Triangles-Fabulous French Bread

Makes 24 appetizers

1 cube (1/2 cup) butter or margarine
4 green onions, finely chopped
1/4 cup parsley, finely chopped
1 cup celery, finely diced
1 tablespoon garlic, finely chopped
1/4 cup sun-dried tomatoes, finely chopped
1/4 cup Kalamata olives, chopped
1/2 cup Parmesan cheese, grated
1 round loaf of sourdough French Bread, unsliced

Melt butter in skillet. Sauté the onions, parsley,celery and garlic until limp. Stir in the sun-dried tomatoes, olives and Parmesan cheese. Stir until well-combined. Slice bread horizontally in half. Spread each half with half of the vegetable mixture. Replace top on bread, wrap in foil and heat 1/2 hour in 350 degree oven. When ready to serve cut each half into 12 wedges. Serve half at a time keeping the other half warm in the oven.

An easy make-ahead appetizer that can also be served as bread with any meal!

Karen Kendall — **Herbert Slater MS, Santa Rosa, CA**

Teriyaki Chicken Wings

Serves 6-8

2 pounds chicken wings or drumettes
1/4 cup Kikkomann Teriyaki Sauce
2/3 cup orange or pineapple juice
1 tablespoon (heaping) orange marmalade

If using whole chicken wings, cut wings at the joint; discard tips. Clean and dry wing sections. Prepare marinade by using 1 measuring cup; first measure teriyaki sauce, fill to 1 cup level with the juice; add the marmalade and mix well so it dissolves. Place wing pieces in a heavy plastic bag; pour marinade over wings; seal tightly. Marinate wings in refrigerator for 24 hours, turning occasionally. Before baking, place wings in a shallow baking dish, reserving marinade for later use. Bake at 350 degrees for 30-45 minutes. Turn wings over every 15 minutes, so they brown evenly. For the last 20 minutes, place marinade in the dish and increase heat to 400 degrees to glaze the wings.

This recipe can be used as a main dish using whole chicken pieces or as a chicken bowl with steamed rice. This is a family favorite!

Laurel Haley — **Fresno HS, Fresno, CA**

Tomato Basil Squares

Serves 8-10

1 package refrigerated pie crust (Pillsbury)
2 cups mozzarella cheese, grated, divided
1/2 cup Parmesan cheese, grated
3 tablespoons fresh basil leaves, chopped
2/3 cup mayonnaise
2 cloves garlic, minced
4 plum tomatoes, thinly sliced

Preheat oven to 375 degrees. Roll out dough onto rectangular baking sheet, creating a giant crust. Sprinkle 1 cup of mozzarella cheese over crust. In medium bowl mix remaining mozzarella, Parmesan, basil, mayonnaise, and garlic. Set aside. Place tomatoes on crust with cheese. Make sure they are side by side and do not overlap. Cover entire crust. Spread mayonnaise mixture on top of tomato cheese crust. Bake for 15-20 minutes, or until bubbly and golden brown.

My friend, JoAnne, shared this recipe with me. Every time I make it everyone raves and wants the recipe.

Vicki Pearl — **Townsend JHS, Chino Hills, CA**

Tulip Sandwiches

Makes about 25

1 loaf white bread
black olive tapanade (purchased at Trader Joe's)
25 Mozzarella slivers
25 Julienne cut strips of Sun dried tomatoes
olive oil
season salt
Parmesan cheese (as topping)

Preheat oven to 425 degrees. Cut the crust off of each slice of bread and throw away the heels of the bread. Working with 2-3 slices at a time to prevent drying spread a moderate amount of tapanade on the bread in a strip formation from corner to corner. Place one piece of mozzarella and one tomato on the tapanade sauce. Moisten the edges of bread with water. Position bread in a diamond shape to your body; pinch together bottom 2 edges to form the tulip shape. Place on a lightly greased cookie sheet. Use a pastry brush to apply olive oil on the outside then sprinkle lightly with season salt and Parmesan cheese. Place in oven to bake for ten minutes or until golden brown in color. Arrange on serving tray, serve warm.

This recipe can use a variety of fillings such as peanut butter and jelly for small kids; pepperoni & cheese with pizza sauce for the teenagers or tarragon cream sauce, roasted chicken and pine nuts for the gourmet. It's an easy, yummy recipe.

Stephanie San Sebastian — **Central HS, Fresno, CA**

Won Ton Appetizers

Makes 2 dozen

1 package won ton wrappers
corn oil for frying
1 pound ground beef
1 onion, minced
1 package taco seasoning
1 small can sliced olives
1 1/2 cup cheddar cheese, grated
1 1/2 cup Jack cheese, grated
sour cream

Preheat oven to 350 degrees. Brush won ton wrappers with corn oil; press into a small muffin tin to form a basket. Bake baskets 5-10 minutes until lightly browned; remove from pan and place on baking sheet. Brown beef with minced onion; drain grease. Add taco seasoning mix and follow directions on package. Remove from heat and place in mixing bowl; add olives and cheese. Fill won ton baskets with meat mixture. Broil until cheese melts; dot with sour cream.

My students love these. The basket shape makes a fun presentation.

Linda Stroup — **Virgin Valley HS, Mesquite, NV**

Zucchini Appetizers

Serves 12-24

3 cups unpared zucchini (4 or 5 small), thinly sliced
1 cup Bisquick mix
1/2 cup onion, finely chopped
1/2 cup Parmesan cheese, grated
2 tablespoons parsley, chopped
1 clove garlic, minced or garlic powder
1/4 teaspoon salt
1/2 teaspoon oregano
dash pepper
4 eggs, slightly beaten
1/2 cup oil

Preheat oven to 350 degrees. Thoroughly mix together all ingredients. Bake in a greased 9 x 13 pan for 25 minutes or until golden brown. Serve warm, cut in squares.

Thank you to Susie Martin for sharing this delicious recipe!

Rhonda Nelson — **Rancho Santa Margarita IS, RSM, CA**

Dips

Artichoke Spinach Dip

Serves 6-8

1 box frozen chopped spinach, thawed
1 cup light sour cream
1/2 cup Parmesan cheese, grated
1 cup part-skim mozzarella cheese, shredded (divided)
8 ounces reduced fat cream cheese, softened
2 cloves garlic, crushed
1/2 teaspoon freshly ground black pepper, plus more as needed
1 teaspoon hot pepper sauce, plus more to taste
1 (14 ounce) can artichoke hearts, drained
carrot sticks, celery sticks and/or baked tortilla strips, for serving

Preheat oven to 350 degrees. Place spinach in paper towels and squeeze out excess liquid. Transfer spinach to a food processor and add the sour cream, Parmesan, 1/2 cup of the mozzarella, the cream cheese, garlic, pepper and hot sauce. Process until just blended but still slightly lumpy. Add artichokes and

pulse to form a chunky mixture. Place in a 1 quart baking dish. Top with remaining mozzarella. Bake until bubbly, about 30 minutes. Serve with carrot sticks, celery sticks or baked tortilla strips.

Donna DeWitz — **Oakmont HS, Roseville, CA**

Baked Spinach & Beef Dip

Serves 24

1 pound ground beef
1 medium onion,chopped
1 (10 ounce) package frozen chopped spinach, well-drained and squeezed dry
1(4 ounce) can mushroom stems and pieces, drained
1 teaspoon garlic salt
1 teaspoon dried basil
1/4 cup butter
1/4 cup all-purpose flour
1/2 teaspoon salt
2 cups milk
1 cup (4 ounces) shredded Monterey Jack or mozzarella cheese

Preheat oven to 350 degrees. In a skillet, cook beef and onion over medium heat until no longer pink; drain. Add the spinach, mushrooms, garlic salt, and basil. Cover and cook for 5 minutes. In a saucepan, melt butter. Stir in the flour and salt until smooth. Gradually add milk. Bring to a boil; cook and stir for 2 minutes or until thickened. Combine sauce and meat mixture in oven safe baking dish; mix well. Sprinkle with cheese. Bake, uncovered, for 20-30 minutes or until heated through. Serve with tortilla chips or crackers.

I've also used this dip as a topping for pasta by mixing it with a can of Italian diced tomatoes.

Jennifer Nelson — **Mendive MS, Sparks, NV**

Bean Dip

Serves 4-6

1 (8 ounce) package cream cheese
1 can (Frito) bean dip
1 (8 ounce) carton sour cream
1 tablespoon chili powder
1/2 bunch green onions, chopped
10 drops Tabasco (or to taste)
1/2 cup (or more) cheese, grated
tortilla chips

Preheat oven to 350 degrees. Mix all ingredients together and top with the cheese. Bake for 15-20 minutes. Serve with tortilla chips.

Quick, easy, and a great party dip!

Beverly Fincher-Ranger — **Carpinteria HS, Carpinteria, CA**

Best Vegetable Dip

Makes 2 cups

1 cup sour cream
1 cup mayonnaise
2 teaspoons green onion, minced
2 teaspoons dill weed
2 teaspoons Bon-apetite seasoning salt

Mix all ingredients together and serve with assorted vegetables.

This has been a family favorite for "YEARS!"

Linda A. Stokes — **Riverton HS, Riverton, UT**

Buffalo Chicken Dip

Serves 10-12

1 pound chicken breast
1 jar Crystal Hot Sauce
1 (8 ounce) block cream cheese
1 jar Marie's Chunky Blue Cheese Dressing
1 bag Colby jack/cheddar cheese, shredded, (divided)

Preheat oven to 350 degrees. Boil chicken breast until cooked. Shred chicken into pieces (fine/chunky depending on how you like it). Pour hot sauce on chicken (as much /little as you like. I use half the bottle so everyone can enjoy it). Marinate chicken and hot sauce for approximately 2 hours in refrigerator. Blend together the cream cheese, blue cheese and 1/2 bag shredded cheese in a bowl. Add marinated chicken to mixture and mix well. Place the mix in a baking dish and put the rest of the shredded cheese on top. Bake for 20 minutes, or until cheese is melted completely. Serve with nacho chips or celery and carrots.

This was passed on to me from my college roommate.
Tastes just like buffalo wings on a celery stick.

Dawn Maceyka — **Great Oak HS, Temecula, CA**

Clam Dip in a Bread Bowl

Makes 1 bread bowl

12 inch round French bread
1 (16 ounce) package cream cheese (half can be sour cream)
2 small cans minced clams
1/2 can clam juice
garlic salt to taste
3 green onions, chopped
2 loaves French bread

Preheat oven to 300 degrees. Combine all ingredients for the dip (will be mushy). Cut the lid off the bread, dig out bread. Put the dip in the bread, replace lid. Wrap in double foil. Bake for 2 hours. Cut up two loaves of French bread to use for dipping.

Mary Deauville — **Prospect HS, Saratoga, CA**

Crab & Artichoke Dip

Serves 8-12

1/2 cup cream cheese, room temperature
1 cup mayonnaise
salt and pepper, to taste
8 ounces canned crab meat
1/2 cup plus 4 tablespoons Parmesan cheese, grated (divided)
6 tablespoons marinated artichokes, drained and chopped
1/4 cup green onions, sliced
1/4 cup celery, diced
2 tablespoons fresh parsley
1 tablespoon red wine vinegar
1 teaspoon Tabasco sauce
1 baguette bread, sliced

Preheat oven to 400 degrees. Beat cream cheese in a large bowl with an electric mixer until smooth. Add mayonnaise and beat until past blended, season with salt and pepper, if desired. Fold in crab meat with rubber spatula. Mix together 1/2 cup Parmesan, artichokes, green onions, celery, parsley, vinegar, and Tabasco. Blend into cream cheese mixture. Pour in 2 cup soufflé dish and top with remaining 4 tablespoons of Parmesan. Bake until cheese melts and serve with baguette slices while hot. Can be prepared a day ahead.

This is one of the best I have tasted. The recipe came from my sister-in-law, Sharon.

Diana Geiger — **Tulare Western HS, Tulare, CA**

Crab & Water Chestnut Dip

Makes 3 cups

1 (6 1/2 ounce) can crab meat
1 (5 ounce) can water chestnuts
2 cups (1 pint) sour cream
2 tablespoons soy sauce
2 tablespoons green onions, minced

Drain and shred crab meat. Mince water chestnuts and drain on paper towels. Combine all ingredients and blend; refrigerate. Serve with mild flavored chips or crackers. Makes 3 cups.

Great to serve at family dinners or at a tail gate party.

Aileen Tanimoto-Matsuura — **Paramount HS, Paramount, CA**

Cranberry Guacamole

Serves 6

1 ripe avocado, pitted, peeled,and coarsely mashed
1/4 cup salsa verde
1 tablespoon and 1 1/2 teaspoons fresh cilantro or
 parsley leaves, chopped
1/2 jalapeño, seeded and deveined, finely chopped
1/2 teaspoon coarse garlic salt
1/3 cup dried cranberries soaked in hot water,
 drained and squeezed dry

Coarsely mash avocados. Fold in remaining ingredients. Guacamole is best made as close to serving as possible. For short-term storage, seal in an airtight container with a piece of plastic wrap against the surface of the guacamole.

A nice change from traditional guacamole - and colorful!

Jill Burnham — **Bloomington HS, Bloomington, CA**

Curry Dip

Serves 4-8

1 cup mayonnaise
2 teaspoons cider vinegar
2 tablespoons chili sauce
2 teaspoons onion, freshly grated
1/2 teaspoon salt
1/8 teaspoon thyme
1/2 teaspoon curry powder
2 teaspoons chives

Mix together all ingredients and refrigerate at least 1/2 hour before serving.

Carol Tower — **West Salem HS, Salem, OR**

Dill Weed Vegetable Dip

Makes about 2 cups

1 cup sour cream
1 cup mayonnaise
2 tablespoons onion, minced
1 tablespoon dill weed
1 teaspoon onion salt
1 teaspoon celery salt

Mix all ingredients and refrigerate. It tastes better if allowed left in the refrigerator for 2-3 hours or even overnight.

From my good friend, Marissa Jones. My students really like it.

Bridella Frenzel — **Yucca Valley HS, Yucca Valley, CA**

Florentine Artichoke Dip

Makes 4 cups

2 (8 ounce) packages cream cheese, softened
1/2 cup mayonnaise
1 (14 ounce) can artichoke hearts, drained and chopped
1 (10 ounce) package frozen chopped spinach, thawed, drained and squeezed dry
1 cup Parmesan cheese, grated
3 cloves garlic, minced
2 tablespoons lemon juice

Preheat oven to 375 degrees. Lightly grease a 7 x 11 inch baking dish. In a medium bowl, mix together the cream cheese and mayonnaise until smooth. Mix in the artichoke hearts, spinach and Parmesan cheese. Season with garlic and lemon juice. Spread evenly into the prepared baking dish. Bake, covered, for 20 minutes. Remove the cover and let the dish bake, uncovered, for 5 more minutes or until the surface is lightly browned.

"I am always asked to make this dip for parties and family gatherings. It is always the first thing to go! Serve it with either crackers, breadsticks or hollow out a round loaf and serve with bread cubes."

Cari Sheridan — **Grace Yokley MS, Ontario, CA**

Guacamole

Makes about 1 1/2 cups

2 avocados, peeled and pitted (choose those that give when you squeeze them. Those that are hard when you buy them never get ripe and have less flavor.)
1 medium tomato, cut into wedges
3 tablespoons onion, cut into wedges (or more, to taste)
1 tablespoon lemon juice
1 teaspoon salt
1/2 teaspoon coarsely ground pepper
4 shakes cayenne pepper (or 4 drops of Tabasco, or a jalapeño pepper—something hot)

Put all of the ingredients together into a blender or food processor. Pulse on and off, pushing the big pieces to the bottom till it is smooth but still has recognizable chunks of tomato. Serve with tortilla chips. Note: Cover in an airtight container or eat immediately. This turns brown quickly. But it still tastes good when it is brown. A layer of mayonnaise or Miracle Whip thinly spread over the top seals out the air but affects the flavor.

The best guacamole I have tasted.

Marilyn Flicki — **North Eugene HS, Eugene, OR**

Homemade Onion Dip

Makes 4 cups

2 yellow onions, peeled and sliced thinly
4 tablespoons butter
1 tablespoon sugar
1 tablespoon balsamic vinegar
pinch of dried rosemary
salt and pepper, to taste
4 ounces cream cheese, softened
1 pint sour cream

Cook the onions slowly in the butter until soft. Sprinkle with the sugar and continue cooking over low heat until onions color. Sprinkle on the vinegar and rosemary and cook until liquid reduces to a syrup. Season with salt and pepper and let cool. Beat cream cheese and stir in sour cream until smooth. Fold onions into sour cream and cheese mixture. Serve with chips.

The best!

Kris Hawkins **Clovis West HS, Fresno, CA**

Hot Pizza Dip

Makes 3 Cups

1(8 ounce) package cream cheese, softened
1 teaspoon Italian seasoning
1 cup mozzarella cheese, shredded
3/4 cup Parmesan cheese, grated
1 (8 ounce) can pizza sauce
2 tablespoons green pepper, chopped
2 tablespoons green onion, thinly sliced
breadsticks or tortilla chips,for serving

In a mixing bowl, beat cream cheese and Italian seasoning. Spread in an ungreased 9 inch microwave-safe pie pan. Combine mozzarella and Parmesan cheeses; sprinkle half over the cream cheese. Top with the pizza sauce, remaining cheese mixture, green pepper and onion. Microwave, uncovered, on high for 3- 4 minutes or until cheese is almost melted, rotating a half turn several times. Let stand for 1-2 minutes. Serve with breadsticks or tortilla chips.

This pizza-flavored dip goes very fast. You might want to make two!

Rebecca Hutchings **Spring Valley HS, Las Vegas, NV**

Hot Spinach Dip

Serves 8-10

2 tablespoons vegetable oil
1 medium onion, chopped
2 tomatoes, chopped
2 tablespoons diced green chiles
1 (10 ounce) package frozen spinach, squeezed dry
7 ounces pepper Jack cheese, grated
1 cup half and half
2 (2.25 ounce) cans sliced black olives
8 ounces cream cheese, cut into 1/2 inch pieces
1 tablespoon red wine vinegar

Preheat oven to 400 degrees. Heat oil in heavy skillet over medium heat; add onions and sauté until softened, stirring occasionally, about 4 minutes. Add tomatoes and chiles and cook 2 minutes. Transfer mixture to large bowl and stir in spinach. Make sure all liquid is squeezed out of spinach. Add jack cheese, half and half, olives, cream cheese, and vinegar. Taste and season with salt and pepper, if needed. Spoon mixture into ovenproof baking dish. Stoneware works great. Bake until dip is bubbly and top is golden, about 35 minutes. Serve with tortilla chips, Fritos, or wheat thins.

I usually use the whole can of chiles. If you like things really hot, you can use jalapeños instead of the chiles.

Lynn Bramham **Taft Union HS, Taft, CA**

Hummus

Serves 6-8

4 garlic cloves, minced and then mashed
2 (15 ounce) cans garbanzo beans (chickpeas), drained and rinsed
2/3 cup tahini, roasted (not raw)
1/3 cup lemon juice, freshly squeezed
1/2 cup water
1/4 cup olive oil
1/2 teaspoon salt
pine nuts, toasted
parsley, chopped for garnish

In a food processor, combine the mashed garlic, garbanzo beans, tahini, lemon juice, water, and olive oil. Process until smooth. Add salt, starting at a half a teaspoon, to taste. Spoon into serving dish and sprinkle with toasted pine nuts and chopped parsley. Serve with crackers, raw dip vegetables such as carrots or celery, or with pita bread. You can cut the pita bread into thin triangles, brush with olive oil and toast for 10 minutes in a 400 degree oven to make pita chips with which to serve the hummus.

This is a recipe from my sister, Karen, and a favorite appetizer at our house!

Linda Johnson **Johansen HS, Modesto, CA**

Killer Dip

Serves 4-6

1 (8 ounce) block cream cheese, softened
1 $1/2$ cups sour cream
1 tablespoon horseradish
1 clove garlic, minced
1 (4 ounce) jar dried beef, chopped

Combine the first three ingredients; mix until smooth. Add garlic and beef; mix thoroughly. Refrigerate overnight. Serve with pretzels, potato chips or crackers.

Stephanie Thomson — **Mesquite HS, Gilbert, AZ**

Layered Dip Italiano

Serves 8-12

1 container soft spreadable cheese, such as goat cheese or flavored cream cheese
1 container pesto
Tapanade (olive salad)
Caponata (eggplant)
sun dried tomatoes, chopped
lettuce for garnish
cracker assortment or sliced baguette for serving
*Purchase a container of spreadable cheese and pesto. Choose one or two of the other ingredients.

Line a small, deep bowl with plastic wrap. (An over sized latte mug works well.) Push several heaping spoonfuls of the spreadable cheese into the bottom of the bowl. Cover with a layer of pesto. Add a layer of one of the other ingredients. Repeat layers. Cover with plastic wrap and refrigerate for an hour. Arrange some lettuce leaves, such as red leaf, on a platter. Unmold the layered dip. Use assorted crackers or sliced baguette to spread the dip.

The ingredients are all store bought. All you need to do is spoon them out of the jars. So simple, so colorful, and so yummy.

Nanci Burkhart-Paulson — **Hueneme HS, Oxnard, CA**

Light Artichoke Dip

Serves 6-10

1 cup light sour cream
1 (14 ounce) can artichoke hearts, drained and coarsely chopped
1 (4.5 ounce) can diced green chiles
4 ounces fresh Parmesan cheese, grated
2 cloves garlic, minced

Preheat oven to 350 degrees, Mix all ingredients together. Bake in small casserole dish 20-25 minutes,uncovered, until lightly browned. Serve immediately with wheat thins or your favorite cracker.

Becky Oppen — **Dana Hills HS, Dana Point, CA**

Mushroom Lover's Pate

Makes 1 1/2 cups

4 tablespoons butter, divided
1/2 pound fresh mushrooms, finely chopped
2 cloves garlic, finely minced
1/4 cup green onions, finely chopped
1/3 cup chicken broth
4 ounces light cream cheese (Neufchatel)
2 tablespoons fresh chives, finely minced
1/4 teaspoon pepper
fresh parsley for garnish
serve with crackers or crostini

In a medium skillet over medium heat, melt 2 tablespoons butter. Add mushrooms and cook 2-3 minutes. Add garlic and green onions; cook 1 minute. Add chicken broth and cook over high heat about 5 minutes or until all the liquid evaporates. Remove from heat; let cool to room temperature. In a medium mixing bowl, with an electric mixer, beat cream cheese and remaining 2 tablespoons butter. Add mushroom mixture, chives and pepper; mix well. Place in a serving bowl. Cover and refrigerate until serving time. Garnish with parsley just before serving.

Mary Makela **Fort Bragg HS, Fort Bragg, CA**

Nancy's Dip

Makes 2 cups

1 pound Jack cheese, melted
1 small can diced green chiles
1 small can white sauce (or make your own)
tortilla chips, for serving
White Sauce:
2 tablespoons butter
2 tablespoons flour
1/4 teaspoon salt
1 cup milk

Melt Jack cheese and add green chiles (I like to microwave them). Add white sauce and heat. Serve hot with tortilla chips. If making your own white sauce; Mix all ingredients in small saucepan and heat, stirring constantly, until smooth.

No event is complete without this dip. Our old family friend, Nancy, gave me this recipe 30 years ago, and it's still everyone's favorite. You can increase ingredients as desired, and it reheats well with just a little added milk (if you manage to have any left!).

Patty Bulat **Rogers MS, Long Beach, CA**

Salmon Dip

Makes 1 1/2 cups

2 (6 ounce) cans premium salmon (no bones or skin)
1 package cream cheese
1 teaspoon garlic, chopped
3 sprigs of green onion
3 drops Liquid Smoke (to taste)
1/2 teaspoon Worcestershire Sauce
pinch of onion powder
pinch of celery salt
black pepper to taste
dill weed for garnish

Blend all ingredients to a paste in a blender. Make 2-3 hours to a day ahead. Sprinkle dill weed on top for decoration.

This is one of my favorite dips that my brother-in-law makes. He's a great chef.

Karen Peters — **Vaca Peña MS, Vacaville, CA**

Salsa Cheese Layered Dip

Serves 14-16

2 (8 ounce) packages cream cheese
1 (16 ounce) jar salsa, divided
2 tablespoons taco seasoning
1 medium green pepper, chopped
1 small red onion, chopped
1 medium tomato, seeded and chopped
2 cups (8 ounces) cheese, shredded
tortilla chips, for serving

Beat cream cheese. Add 1 cup salsa; mix. Add taco seasoning; mix. Spread on 12-inch serving plate. Sprinkle with green pepper, onion, and tomato. Top with remaining salsa, sprinkle with cheese. Serve with chips.

This is a great party dip. A great alternative to layered bean dip.

Jeanette Atkinson — **Legacy HS, North Las Vegas, NV**

Seven Layer Bean Dip

Serves 12

1 (16 ounce) can refried beans
1 avocado, mashed
3/4 cup sour cream
3/4 cup cheddar cheese, grated
1/2 cup chunky salsa, drained; or 1 tomato, chopped
1 (small) can chopped olives
1 (small) can diced Ortega chiles

Spread beans on a dinner size plate and heat in microwave until warm, approximately 1 minute. Spread with remaining ingredients in order given. Serve with tortilla chips.

Cindy Bowman — **McFarland HS, McFarland, CA**

Seven-Layer Dip

Makes a lot

1 pound ground beef or ground turkey
Lawry's taco seasoning
2 avocados
3 or 4 medium tomatoes, chopped
2 large onions, chopped
1/2 bunch medium size cilantro
1 (16 ounce) container sour cream, (approximately 2 cups)
1 pound cheddar cheese, shredded
tortilla chips for serving

Preheat oven to 325 degrees. Brown meat and add the taco seasoning as instructed on the packet. Place in the bottom of a 9 x 12 casserole dish. This is the bottom layer. Next peel and mash avocados and mix well with the tomatoes, onion and cilantro. Spread mixture on top of the meat. Layer your choice of sour cream and finally top with the cheese. Bake for about 20 minutes. Let it cool and serve with chips.

This can be a meal all it's own or a great appetizer for Super Bowl Sunday.

Leah Brown — **Marina HS, Huntington Beach, CA**

Sheepherder's Bread Dip

Serves 8

1 round loaf Sheepherder's bread, unsliced
1 (8 ounce) package cream cheese, softened
2 tablespoons milk
1 (2.5 ounce) jar chipped beef, chopped
2 tablespoons onion, finely minced
1/8 teaspoon pepper
1/2 cup sour cream
1/2 cup walnuts or almonds, chopped
vegetables, cut up for dipping

Preheat oven to 250 degrees. Slice off the top of Sheepherder's bread; save top. Hollow out loaf, saving bread for dipping. Mix together remaining ingredients and place inside hollowed out loaf. Bake for 2 hours. Leave top off while baking. Serve with chunks of bread and vegetables.

I usually double the recipe, and it really fills the bread bowl.
Everyone LOVES this dip!

Ruth Schletewitz — **Rafer Johnson JHS, Kingsburg, CA**

Shrimp Cheese Dip

Serves 12

1/2 pound cheddar cheese, shredded
1 can cream of shrimp soup, or cream of mushroom soup
1 can shrimp
green onions, chopped, to taste
1/2 teaspoon garlic salt, to taste

Heat the cheese and soup in a pan on low or in the microwave. Add shrimp, onions, and garlic. Serve as a dip for veggies or bread sticks.

My favorite for a Christmas buffet.

Sheri Rader — Chaparral HS, Las Vegas, NV

Shrimp Dip

Serves 12-24

2 (8 ounce) packages cream cheese, softened
2 cups Best Foods Mayonnaise
2 cans shrimp, drained
1 bunch green onions, chopped
2 tablespoons lemon juice
1 tablespoon Worcestershire sauce

Use an electric mixer to blend the cream cheese and mayonnaise together. Mix in the remaining ingredients. Chill for 2-3 hours then serve.

You can serve this with bread, vegetables, crackers, or potato chips!

Jennifer Hill — Kearns HS, Kearns, UT

Smoked Salmon Dip

Makes 1 1/2 cups

4 ounces cream cheese, softened
3 tablespoons mayonnaise
2 tablespoons sour cream
juice of 2 lemons
dash Worcestershire sauce
dash Mrs. Dash seasoning
4 ounces smoked salmon, crumbled into small pieces, without bones or skin
1 teaspoon dill weed, or to taste

Mix all ingredients except the salmon until smooth. Add the crumbled salmon gently. Serve cold with crackers or pita bread. This can be made with unsmoked canned salmon and is also delicious.

This recipe was served for a New Years celebration and went over very well.

Sandy Ransom — Tehachapi HS, Tehachapi, CA

Sun-Dried Tomato Dip

Makes 2 cups

1 jar sun-dried tomatoes in oil
4 cloves garlic
1/2 teaspoon pepper
1/2 teaspoon salt
2 teaspoons lemon juice
1 cup fresh basil leaves
2 tablespoons Parmesan cheese
olive oil to taste (optional)

Drain about 1/4 of the oil off the tomatoes. Combine all ingredients in a food processor. Pulse until evenly chopped. Adjust texture with olive oil to taste. Serve as a dip or a spread on French bread rounds or crackers.

This delicious dip recipe was given to me by my daughter-in-law, Carolyn Wayland. We enjoy this at family gatherings. It is very fresh.

Joan Wayland — **O. W. Holmes JHS, Davis, CA**

Super Bowl Party Dip

Makes 2 cups

2 packages of Jimmy Dean Sausage
1 onion, chopped
3 large packages cream cheese
1 can green chiles

Brown sausage and onion. Mix in cream cheese and chiles. Pour in a crock pot and serve warm.

Always a big hit at any party.

Linda Brayton — **Grace Davis HS, Modesto, CA**

Super Simple Artichoke Dip

Serves 6-8

1 cup mayonnaise
1 cup Parmesan cheese
1 can artichoke hearts, drained (marinated or plain)
3-4 cloves of garlic, crushed
salt and pepper, to taste

In an oven safe dish (works best if it is relatively flat), mix mayonnaise, cheese, artichoke hearts, and garlic until thoroughly combined. Add a few dashes of salt and pepper and spread into pan (a thin layer - about 3/4 inch works best). Broil about 5 minutes, until the top is lightly browned. Remove from broiler carefully and serve warm with crackers or toasted bread pieces.

The recipe is easily doubled or tripled for more people. This is a favorite at parties. Tastes great warm, and even after it cools down; it's still pretty yummy!!

Holly Hall — **West HS, Torrance, CA**

The Trawler's Famous Crab Dip

Makes About 3 cups

1 1/4 cups mayonnaise
1 cup crab meat
1/2 cup sharp cheddar cheese, finely grated
1 teaspoon horseradish
1/4 cup French Dressing

Place all ingredients in a bowl and mix together; chill until ready to serve. Serve with assorted snack crackers. For an extra tang, don't be afraid to add more horseradish or French dressing to suit personal taste.

Delicious before dinner treat from one of South Carolina's famous restaurants.

Anne Hawes — **Cottonwood HS, Murray, UT**

Zippy Cranberry Dip

Serves 10-12

1 pound fresh cranberries
1 cup water
sprinkle of salt
2 cups sugar
potato chips, Frito Scoops, or your favorite chips

Wash and sort fresh cranberries. Place in a saucepan, add water and salt, bring to a boil. Cook only until cranberries begin to pop. Remove from heat and force cranberries through a sieve to remove seeds. Return puree to saucepan and add sugar. Bring to a boil. Pour into a mold. Chill until set. Remove from mold just before serving.

A family favorite for Thanksgiving and Christmas.
(Note: Overcooking cranberries causes bitterness.)

Mary Lash — **Paramount HS, Paramount, CA**

Salsas

California Cowboy Caviar

Makes 3 cups

4 tablespoons red wine vinegar
1/4 teaspoon Tabasco sauce; any hot sauce, to taste
3 tablespoons olive oil
1 clove garlic, minced
1/4 teaspoon salt, to taste
1/8 teaspoon pepper, to taste
1 avocado, cut into 1/2 inch cubes
1 (15 ounce) can black eyed peas, rinsed and drained
1 (11 ounce) can corn kernels
2-3 green onions, thinly sliced
2 tablespoons cilantro, minced
8 ounces roma tomatoes, seeded and chopped
tortilla chips or pita chips

In a large bowl mix vinegar, hot sauce, oil, garlic, salt and pepper. Add the cubed avocado and mix gently to coat. Add the peas, corn, onions, cilantro and tomatoes to the avocado mixture and mix gently. Adjust taste with hot sauce, salt and pepper. Serve with tortilla chips or pita chips.

This is also great served with fresh fish or in fish tacos.
In Texas this is served on New Year's Day to bring good luck.

Janice Tuttle — **Mills HS, Millbrae, CA**

Fresh Melon Salsa

Serves 6-12

1 small cantaloupe, dice or shaped into small balls
1 small honeydew melon, diced or shaped into small balls
2 tablespoons brown sugar
1-3 Serrano chiles, minced
1 lime, squeezed for juice
1 clove of garlic, mashed (optional)
3 tablespoons fresh mint (optional)

Combine all ingredients and gently toss. Adjust seasoning and refrigerate.

Lisa Harris — **Sonora HS, La Habra, CA**

Jalapeño Salsa or Grilled Flank Steak Marinade

Makes approximately 1 1/2 cups

1 jalapeño
1/4 bunch cilantro
2 tablespoons ground cumin
3 limes, juiced
2 ounces olive oil
2 gloves garlic, minced or chopped
salt and pepper to taste
(pinch of brown sugar if it gets too hot)

Measure all ingredients in blender; blend until smooth. Bake some flour tortillas, cut in strips or wedges, and use for scooping this flavorful dip. It is muy caliente!

This salsa/marinade does not need to be heated-it has it's own heat!
Great flavors enhance any beef meal. This recipe came from CSCA in Pasadena.
You be the Iron Chef and create your own signature taste.

Barbara Allen — **Rueben S. Ayala HS, Chino Hills, CA**

California Wrap-its

Serves 6

1 cup ranch salad dressing
8 ounces cream cheese, softened
4 large (10-inch) flour tortillas, warmed
10 ounces turkey breast slices
10 ounces Monterey Jack cheese and/or Cheddar Cheese, sliced
2 large Fresh California avocados, peeled, sliced thinly
2 medium tomatoes, sliced thinly
alfalfa sprouts, optional

Blend together dressing and cream cheese. Spread evenly on tortillas. Evenly layer turkey, cheese, avocados, tomatoes and sprouts on tortillas, leaving a 1-inch border. Fold the bottom edge toward the center and firmly roll away from you until completely wrapped. Place seam side down and slice.

Photo and recipe courtesy of California Fresh Avocado Commission

Ham & Noodle Tarts

Makes 36

1/4 pound sliced ham
4 ounces Swiss cheese
3 green onions
1 cup uncooked alphabet noodles or small egg noodles
3 eggs
1 1/2 cups half and half
1 teaspoon salt
1/8 teaspoon ground nutmeg

Heat oven to 350 degrees F. Grease 36 mini (or 12 regular) muffin pan cups generously. Set aside. Chop ham, cheese and green onions finely; set aside. Cook noodles following label directions, just to the al dente state; drain. Mix drained noodles into ham mixture. Divide mixture among the muffin pan cups (Bake tarts in 3 batches if there is only 1 pan). In a medium bowl, beat eggs slightly, stir in half and half, salt and nutmeg. Spoon liquid mixture over the ham mixture in muffin pans, dividing evenly among them. Bake for 35 minutes. Ease out of pan gently, using a sharp knife around the edge if necessary. Transfer to warm serving platter; serve piping hot. *Make-ahead tip:* Tarts may be refrigerated, covered, for up to 3 days before serving. Reheat in a 350 degrees F. oven until hot, about 10 minutes.

Recipe and photo courtesy of National Pork Board

California Wrap-its

Ham & Noodle Tarts

Wisconsin Blue Cheese Balls with Winter Fruit

Wisconsin Blue Cheese Balls with Winter Fruit

Makes 30

30 dried apricots
Water
4 teaspoons pure vanilla extract
2/3 cup coarsely chopped pecans
4 ounces Cream Cheese cut in chunks and room temperature
3 ounces (3/4 cup) Wisconsin Blue cheese, crumbled
1 tablespoon French brandy*
1/2 tablespoon grated yellow onion

Place the apricots in a sauce pan. Add water barely to cover. Stir in vanilla. Bring the apricots to a boil, uncovered, and simmer until tender, 1-4 minutes, depending on the dryness of the apricots. Test with a fork. The apricots should be tender but not limp. Drain and dry well. Set aside. Preheat the oven to 375°. Spread the pecans on a baking sheet. Toast the pecans for 4-5 minutes, until aromatic. Stir after 2 minutes and watch so the nuts do not scorch. Remove and pour pecans on waxed paper to cool. Whirl the pecans in a blender or food processor until very fine. Set aside. Place the Cream Cheese, Wisconsin Blue cheese and brandy in the bowl of a food processor. Pulse until all ingredients are well blended. Add the onion and pulse briefly to incorporate. (You may also blend the mixture in the bowl of an electric mixer.) Remove mixture to a bowl and refrigerate at least 2 hours. Remove cheese mixture from refrigerator. Form miniature balls and dip tops in pecans. Place on an apricot, nut side up. Repeat until all mixture is used. The mixture is soft – if too soft, spoon onto apricots, rounding the top and sprinkle with apricots. Makes about 30 miniature balls. This mixture is a terrific filling for stewed dried plums (prunes) and Majool dates. Make a party plate with all winter fruits – apricots, dried plums and dates – for variety. *If a nonalcoholic mixture is preferred, substitute sherry extract. Start with 1/4 teaspoon and add to taste.

Recipe and photo courtesy of Wisconsin Milk Marketing Board

Mango Salsa

Makes approximately 2 1/2 cups

1-2 mangos, peeled and diced;
start with 1, but 2 is better, ripe but not too soft
1/2 large red onion, diced
apple cider vinegar, not so much as to make the recipe too liquid
1/4 bunch cilantro, remove and chop leaves only
2 tablespoons brown sugar
1-2 Habanero peppers, finely chopped,
depending on the size and the amount of heat you like
(wear gloves or be sure to wash hands completely)

Mix ingredients, taste, adjust to your preference and enjoy! The flavors of onion and mango are amazing together. You decide how much of each ingredient depending on what you like. You be the Iron Chef! This can be a chunky salsa depending on how fine you dice the mango and onion. This is great on ham or chicken or just with chips. It has a hot and spicy, sweet and sour taste.

I always get a request for this recipe from friends. Everyone is delighted with the fantastic flavor boost it gives any food. The California School of Culinary Arts in Pasadena shared this recipe during an Educator Appreciation Day. A big thanks to CSCA!

Barbara Allen **Rueben S. Ayala HS, Chino Hills, CA**

Texas Caviar

Serves 6-10

2 cans black beans, drained and washed
1 can shoepeg corn
2 cans diced tomatoes with green chiles
1 red pepper
1 yellow pepper
1 bunch green onions
1 bunch cilantro
1/2 teaspoon garlic (powder, salt or fresh)
1/8 teaspoon cayenne pepper

Wash vegetables and cut or dice as needed. Mix all ingredients together and serve with tortilla chips.

This is my family's favorite salsa, and it is really easy to make.

Camille Hicks **Riverton HS, Riverton, UT**

Contributor Index

C

D

E

S

T

V

Recipe Index

Cold Appetizers

Hot Appetizers

Great Beginnings

Dips

Salsas

FLIP OVER FOR

Great Beginnings

FLIP OVER FOR

Sweet Endings